Dylan's recent tour was his first extended public appearance since 1966. Pickering shows why he did it and what it was like: the pop star speaking to his audience like a Rabbi, entertaining us with wonderful stories, teaching us a lesson, but moving us with the truth about who we are and how we feel.

Pickering's insights help us better to enjoy Dylan. His point of view shows us why Dylan means so much to so many people. Designed by Jon Goodchild, who did *The Rolling Stones*, **Bob Dylan: Approximately** is both an education and a treat.

Stephen Pickering

Then the great Rabbi Israel Ba'al Shem-Tov saw misfortune threatening the Jews, it was his custom to go into a certain part of the forest to meditate. There he would light a fire, say a special prayer, and the miracle would be accomplished, and the misfortune averted.

Later, when his disciple, the celebrated Magid of Mezritch, had occasion, for the same reason, to intercede with heaven, he would go to the same place in the forest and say: "Master of the Universe, listen! I do not know how to light the fire, but I am still able to say the prayer." And again the miracle would be accomplished.

Still later, Rabbi Moshe-Leib of Sasov, in order to save his people once more, would go into the forest and say: "I do not know how to light the fire, I do not know the prayer, but I know the place and this must be sufficient." It was sufficient and the miracle was accomplished.

Then it fell to Rabbi Israel of Rizhyn to overcome misfortune. Sitting in his armchair, his head in his hands, he spoke to God: "I am unable to light the fire and I do not know the prayer; I cannot even find the place in the forest. All I can do is to tell the story, and this must be sufficient." And it was sufficient.

God made man because He loves stories.

—Rabbi Israel of Rishin, as retold by Elie Wiesel in *The Gates of the Forest*, trans. Frances Frenaye (New York: Holt, Rinehart & Winston, 1966).

ALSO BY STEPHEN PICKERING

Editor (and contributing author):
Dylan: A Commemoration
Praxis One: Existence, Men, and
    Realities
Aggadah: Studies in Bob Dylan and
    Torah Judaism
Kavvanah: Mystic Steps and Dylaneutics
Bob Dylan: Tour 1974 (out of print)

Author:
"Knockin' on Heaven's Door" and
    "Billy": A Jewish Speculation

BOB DYLAN APPROXIMATELY

A Portrait of the Jewish Poet in Search of God

A Midrash

STEPHEN PICKERING
Chofetz Chaim Ben-Avraham

Photography by George Gruel, Peter Vogl and others
Designed by Jon Goodchild
Special Editorial Assistance by H. Samuel Fleishmann

David McKay Company, Inc. New York

Cloth 0-679-50493-1
ISBN: Paper 0-679-50529-6
Library of Congress
    Catalog Card Number: 74-29325
Manufactured in the United States of America

This book, written by a religious Jew, is directed toward *all* who—in time of pain, in moments of joy—have asked questions and, in the asking, have formulated new, experiential answers. Many times one may be swayed by the Breath moving, unseen, behind an autumn rain. Thus, one has been a mystic-without-vehicle. This is the author's fifth book on Bob Dylan, and to those listed below, who gave time and talent, a special word of thanks:

Hudson Brack and Lynn Hrabko.
Bob Dylan, for reading the original review of
    Planet Waves, and for the kind words in
    Chicago and St. Louis.
Martin Essayan, for sharing Armenian visions.
Ethan and Greta Hamm, for many things.
David Meltzer, for lights and doorways.
Joel Rosenberg, for stories.
Anthony Scaduto, for opening doors.
Joel Siegel, for not forgetting that you, too, are a
    Jew.
Robert Somma of *Fusion*.
Rob West, for that Jesuit sign in your hat in Boston.
Diane Richardson; Barry Feinstein, for kind
    words; Rob Fraboni; Clyde and Jeanne
    Herr; Roberta Richards of Toronto; Leslie,
    my brother; Leb Zindel ben-Z'av, for his
    frustrated fangs; Maureen Orth; Urban
    Gwerder; Ko Lankester of Holland.

And, on behalf of George Gruel, to Barbara Werney; Todd Weinstein; Mrs. Helen Gruel; David Seals; Bill Graham; George Phillips and Barbara Vogl.

Photographic Contributions by: John Collier, Danny Connolly, Steve Epeneter, Bob Gruen, Laura Greenwood, Urban Gwerder, Robb Lawrence, Michael Lessner, Charles Osgood, Neal Preston, Chuck Pulin, Vernon Shibla, Joseph Sia, Ronald Sweering and Art Usherson.

Grateful Acknowledgment is made for permission to reprint from the following:

Rabbi Jacob Agus, for excerpts from *Banner of Jerusalem: The Life, Times, and Thought of Abraham Isaac Kuk* (Bloch Publishing Co.), © 1946, 1972 by Rabbi Jacob B. Agus. **Atheneum Publishers**, for excerpts from Andre Schwarz-Bart, *The Last Of the Just*, trans. Stephen Becker (Atheneum Publishers), © 1960 by Atheneum Publishers. **Rabbi Ben Zion Bokser**, for excerpts from a review of Alter B. Z. Metzger's translation of Rav A. I. Kuk's *Orot Ha-Teshuvah*, published in the Summer 1969 issue of *Conservative Judaism*. © 1969 by Rabbi Ben Zion Bokser. **Farrar, Straus & Giroux Inc**, for excerpts from *Israel: An Echo Of Eternity* by Rabbi Abraham Joshua Heschel, © 1967, 1968, 1969 by Abraham Joshua Heschel; for excerpts from *Man Is Not Alone* by Rabbi Abraham Joshua Heschel, © 1951 by Abraham Joshua Heschel. **Holt, Rinehart and Winston Inc**, for excerpts from *The Gates of The Forest* by Elie Wiesel, trans. Frances Frenaye. © 1966 by Holt, Rinehart and Winston Inc. **The Joint Prayer Book Commission, The Rabbinical Assembly** and **The United Synagogue of America**, for an excerpt from a poem by Rav A. I. Kuk, trans. Morris Silverman, in *Sabbath and Festival Prayer*, ed. Morris Silverman, © 1946, 1973 by The Rabbinical Assembly and by The United Synagogue of America. **Random House Inc**, for excerpts from *One Generation After* by Elie Wiesel, © 1965, 1967, 1970 by Elie Wiesel. **Anthony Scaduto**, for excerpt from *Bob Dylan: An Intimate Biography* (Grosset and Dunlap), © 1971, 1973 by Anthony Scaduto. **Schocken Books Inc,** for excerpts from *Tales of the Hasidim: Early Masters*, by Martin Buber, © 1947 by Schocken Books Inc. **Ralph J. Gleason,** for excerpts from articles in *San Francisco Chronicle*, copyrighted 1964 and 1965.

For a listing and copyright information for all songs quoted in this book, see page 208.

Introduction

"I lost my way in a narrow passage way, and I bumped into the Wailing Wall."—Bob Dylan to Maureen Orth of *Newsweek* (Chicago, 3 January 1974).

Bob Dylan is a post-Holocaust Jewish voice, searching for and rediscovering the manifestations of God. He has told me: "I have never forgotten my roots. I am a Jew."

The Jewish people began their history as a "tribe" of wanderers who evolved into spiritual, as well as physical, nomads. The Rabbis teach us: on Mount Sinai, Moses not only saw the letters of Torah, but also heard the silence (the hidden meanings) between the letters. The Talmud further teaches: when Moses descended from Mount Sinai and saw the people prostrate before the Golden Calf, he shattered the first set of Tablets, the first letters and silences of Torah.

Bob Dylan is one of a succession of Jewish mystics—Yitzhak Luria, Avraham ben Samuel Abulafia, Moses Cordovero, Rav Avraham Yitzhak Kuk, Rav Schneur Zalman, Rav Arele Roth, Rav Nachman of Bratzlav, and others of blessed memory—who have searched for, and tried to reintegrate, that fractured original vision: rediscovering the silences, and "raising the sparks" contained within each soul "to the fire." Poets are given gifts of understanding, teaches one rabbinic sage in the Zohar, denied even to angels.

This book is a *midrash*, a searching out, through description and commentary, of Bob Dylan's 1974, North American tour. This book presents an authentic perspective of Dylan—as a Jew.

The Jew's role in history has been as a witness, a conscience for mankind, a reminder of the Covenant at Sinai. The Jew sustains the unity of the Name, the bridge between Sinai and our times. While being "the fewest of all the nations" (*ha'm'at mikol ha'amim*), Jews have sought a glimpse of *orot ha'kodesh*, the supernal lights of holiness.

In Bob Dylan's richly symbolic poetry are specific Jewish themes, root experiences consistent with centuries of thought and tradition. First: the Covenant at Sinai, the giving of Torah; the reality of the "binding of the soul" (the phrase is used by Dylan in "WEDDING SONG") to God. This "binding" affirms the sovereignty of the Father of Night, the rejection of wicked messengers, the acceptance of the emanations of God to

"all the families of the earth" (Genesis 12:3). Secondly, *teshuvah* (returning). Assailed with questions and the darkness of spiritual eclipse, Bob Dylan seeks the lights shimmering in *halakhah*, Torah's paths which demand active thought and deed. Thirdly, there is *tefillah* (prayer): Bob Dylan's turning from the experiences of nightmarish exile to hope, to cry out (*za'ak*, as in Judges 3:9 and "I SHALL BE RELEASED"); to lift up (*nasa*), to climb the soul's ladder (as in "FOREVER YOUNG" and Jeremiah 7:16); to pour out one's heart (*shafakh lev*, as in Psalm 62:9 and "WICKED MESSENGER"). Prayer, teaches the Talmud (Berakot 29b–30a), is not a pleading for one's self, but for all people; it is service of the heart. Fourth, *shirah* (song): poetry commingled with *tefillah*; together, they play and twist to express the Ineffable, evoking a quality called by Rav Abraham Joshua Heschel, of blessed memory, "radical surprise." Finally: the soul (*nefesh*), the breath which God, blessed be He, blew into our essences, reflected in Dylan's tortuous cycles of eclipse ("CHIMES OF FREEDOM") and tenderness ("TO RAMONA" and "WEDDING SONG"), his necessary solitude ("NOTHING WAS DELIVERED" and "DIRGE").

Music and prayer are at the heart of the Jewish soul. We cannot speak to God, as He is beyond grasp (*Ein Sof*, without limit); but man's words and melodies do influence His emanation of *hesed* (loving-kindness). We contemplate the hidden potencies of words, of letters, giving forth (as does Bob Dylan) incantations to the hiddenness of existence. By giving melody to his prayers, Dylan strengthens an awareness of the Jew's commitment to God. Through Talmud and commentaries, we discover the duties and highways the soul must travel; but, through the poetry of kabbalah (the Jewish mystical traditions), we discover the hidden melody of the letters.

King David believed the Torah to be a song (Psalm 119:54). By singing his prayers, Bob Dylan conjures the currents of the soul. Bob Dylan's prayer/poems reflect exile and the promise of *teshuvah*, the song contained in each encounter of one's life. As one's soul ascends the ladder of awareness, "the more exalted its music," taught Nachman of Bratzlav. The Zohar instructs that, in Heaven, there are doors which can only be opened with song. The kabbalists (including the "Lubavitcher" Hasidim, whose influence upon Dylan since 1967 is important) have taught: the soul can touch its inner, divine spark through song, the "extended tune" (*l'meshokh niggunim*), that singing must precede *teshuvah*.

The sacred Zohar also instructs that in singing, serving Him with gladness, we draw closer to the Light. As a Jewish voice, whose most recent work in *Planet Waves* is a reflection of the ten expressions of prayer (the album is comprised of ten songs, excluding the out-take of "FOREVER YOUNG"), Bob Dylan has been unique: reaching millions of people, giving melody to prayers which have not yet become devout liturgies.

Bob Dylan's poetry centers upon God, upon Heaven (paths to the Gates of Eden, where man will knock on Heaven's door), upon the extant Jewish messianic tradition. His sense of impending apocalypse (the dialectical struggle between darkness and light) burns into the Jewish heart. In his moral anger, his ethical monotheism, Bob Dylan is a Jewish voice aware of the struggles which can tear apart the heart: what one ought to do as opposed to what one wants to do. Dylan has, in "WEDDING SONG," admitted that it was never his "intention to sound the battle charge." However, the fire is in him like Jeremiah: he cannot be silent.

Dylan grew up in Hibbing, Minnesota, where there lived many devout Jews. At his *bar mitzvah* (22 May 1954), they heard him read from the *haftorah* (a selection of readings from the Prophets) in Hebrew, and listened to his talk on the moral duty of the Jew. Dylan "conducted the ceremony beautifully," a witness recalls. "His home was religious." The Jews of Hibbing worshipped and prayed at Agudath Achim Synagogue; and Dylan's *bar mitzvah* there, one learns, "leaned more toward orthodox." Dylan then left the Midwest, encountering a society not permeated with Torah, but nurturing violence; a society whose "tongue could not speak but only flatter" ("THE WICKED MESSENGER").

The Jewish mystics frown upon monasticism, the total isolation from others. One must be active in one's community, one must worship with others. The kabbalist, alone and contemplative, is under an obligation to share his teachings; "all the forces will be transformed" (writes the author of *Kaf Ha-Ketoreth*), the soul will rediscover the latent fires of Torah. Then—and only then—can the poet, replenished in the foundation of his family, talk to his "brothers in the flood" (as Dylan writes in the jacket notes of *Planet Waves*).

Today: Bob Dylan prays and shares his prayers . . . he has studied with Rav Shlomo Friefeld of Far Rockaway, New York (a most learned man) . . . he does not eat pork . . . as did Dylan, his children have gone to a *religious* Jewish summer camp . . . he has contributed to Israel . . . with his wife, in 1971 he visited the Mount Zion Yeshiva in Israel . . . at one time (according to Rabbi Richard Rocklin of Charlotte, North Carolina) he contemplated renting an apartment in

Jerusalem . . . and, after several visits to Israel, he applied for membership on a kibbutz (according to the kibbutz's secretary, they delayed in answering his application and never heard from him again) . . .

Bob Dylan utilized Tour 1974 to quicken the restoration of inner covenants: each concert reflected the tension and dialogue of his own *tikkun*, or inner re-integration. He sang as a Jewish soul experiencing both the joy and burden of being a protagonist in the struggle to restore the kingdom of Heaven to this existence. Like a *rebbe* talking to his students, he gave us a distillation of his sources and experiences over a span of

twelve years. Everything: the rage and disappointment and hope.

The Talmud speaks of two messiahs, two deliverers: one of the house of Jacob, one of the house of David. One of war, another of peace. The completion of *tikkun*, therefore, means the end of history, and the beginning of an age of non-temporality. Bob Dylan, with us all, struggles to make prayer a "chariot" for the soul's ascent to *Ein Sof*. We await that, teaches the Talmud, which will come when one least expects it: the beginning of the messianic era. Such an era will be radically different in one aspect, wrote Maimonides: men shall be free. The paradox for Bob Dylan: being inwardly free in an age which throws the soul toward suicide. Freedom of the soul must be renewed again and again. Tradition tells us that the Messiah is at the gates of Jerusalem, binding those who are wounded. When will he come? asks a young man in the Talmud. He will come, says the Psalmist (Psalm 95:7), if we will only listen to His voice.

To hear, to listen, to answer, Bob Dylan cries out, man must be free. A Jewish slave, the Talmud tells us, chose to remain a slave and was punished by having his ear disfigured. Why? The Talmud teaches that God said: Because it was the ear which heard Me say upon Mount Sinai, "Unto Me are the children of Israel servants, but not servants of My servants." In a commentary to Exodus 21:6, the great sage, Simeon ben Judah ha-Nasi reached a similar conclusion: the ear has to be placed against the doorpost of heaven. If the Jew does not knock on heaven's door, then self-imposed slavery is a desecration of the soul which reflects His image.

It is my fervent wish that the quotations and reflections on Bob Dylan's Jewish visions in this volume will show Bob Dylan in the spirit of his own unfolding, will assist the reader in the process of his own *tikkun*.

—S.P.

חפץ ח"ם בן אברהם

1 October 1974/
15 Tishri 5735

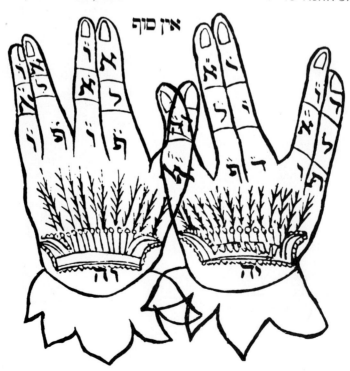

Prologue

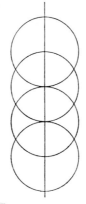

Narrative

Friday, 2 November 1973, a sunny, slightly windy day in the San Francisco Bay Area. The announcement was more than words typed by one of Mr. Bill Graham's secretaries: a hope was realized, a dream was about to unfold. "Singer Bob Dylan will present his first Bay Area concerts in eight years on Monday night, February 11." The atmosphere swirling about the office of Mr. Graham's FM Productions was tense after the announcement, and even his employees, in some instances, were caught by surprise. Graham soon departed by airplane from San Francisco, telling them, "I'm off to see God" (as Herb Caen, the newspaper columnist, quoted him at the time). Arrangements for concert sites were not yet complete, and his office would only tell the press that Chicago, 3 January 1974, would be the beginning, and Los Angeles, 14 February 1974, the completion.

"All I ask," said Bob Dylan to Bill Graham, "is that you keep everything low-key." Designs for concert posters were developed, then abandoned: a horizon with a rising sun; a nineteenth-century train, with one of the car's sides stating, "Bob Dylan/The Band, Tour 74".

Those seeking more information were thwarted by Mr. Graham's unrelenting desire to maintain calm. Throughout November, the news of the tour precipitated expectations and thought. Ticket purchase (except in a few cases) was to be by mail order only; only letters postmarked after midnight, 2 December 1973, would be accepted. David Geffen, chairman of Elektra-Asylum Records, simultaneously denied the existence of a Dylan/The Band album (which had already been recorded, 5, 6 and 9 November, at West Los Angeles' Village Recorder), or that his company had signed Mr. Dylan. Geffen's understandable reluctance to be absorbed by the media rumor-machine reflected the concern of everyone connected with the planning of the tour.

"After an eight-year hiatus," a member of Columbia Broadcasting System said to Ian Dove, of the *New York Times*, a week after the announcement of the tour, "there's a whole new generation out there." With many of the final arrangements for halls still pending, it was difficult to judge the nature of the "generation out there." Radicalism was shattered both by impotence before a gargantuan political machine, and by historical short-sightedness. It was easy to assume the role of "revolutionary" on the steps of a revolution-lacking university, to talk of "liberation." Only a few writers—Allen Ginsberg, Hal Draper, Tom Hayden and Michael McClure—grasped that a government which nepalmed and murdered entire peoples would not change its positions on arguments of "morality."

Everything had changed after 1967. Now the music world was industrialized, while radical spokesmen were being tried by the government. Confusion was (and still is) rampant. Before Bob Dylan offered his intrinsically Jewish spirituality in poetry, those purchasing records wore saddle shoes and crinolines, had to wash dishes for a small allowance. The music fan magazines had been in their infancies. Now, in 1974, ten of these publications (*Fave!*, *16*, *Tiger Beat*, among others) struggle for the attention and finances of those who

are apolitical, those who, unlike the readers of *Rolling Stone* and *Fusion*, saturate themselves with television's moon-glow, sea-shell fantasies and music. The word in the industry is "matched product," and those behind these magazines realize that their teenage audience buys more records than its older brothers and sisters. Their younger "artists" fluff their hair, write advice columns, give away their clothes, and sell posters and order blanks. Fascism has become fashionable, as witnessed, for example, by the media's silence toward the American Indian Movement.

Thus, the first few weeks after the announcement of the tour brought both excitement and contemplations. A private jet, Starship I (equipped with living quarters, vegetarian and kosher-food courses), was being readied for departure. Newspaper gossip columnists in Hollywood were accusing Dylan of fear, of being a veritable vegetable. Those

ART USHERSON. MARIPOSA, 1972

having a firmer grip on their minds were quietly preparing themselves for a prodigious excursion into reality. "Everybody had forgotten about the possibility of Bob Dylan and The Band ever playing together again," Robbie Robertson said in November. "For a long time, everybody expected us to do it and we never did. So, now we do it and it catches everybody off guard. That really makes it interesting from our side of it and you have to be interested or it isn't any good."

Days passed in November. A concert scheduled for the San Diego Sports Arena, 8 February, was cancelled after being rescheduled for 12 February. Still, little information was available. "We wanted to keep this a secret and avoid the hysteria as long as possible," said Bill Graham to Edith M. Ledere of the Associated Press. "I think this will be the largest cross section of music lovers that I'd

ever expect to see at a concert," Mr. Graham later predicted.

Earlier, during the summer, Robbie Robertson and Dylan had agreed that the tour would be remarkably different than that of Europe in early 1966, when the audiences (particularly at London's Royal Albert Hall and in Paris) were vicious in their receptions. Robertson had already talked with Bill Graham and David Geffen, and believed them to be capable of organizing a tour which, at best, would be hectic and exhilarating. After moving to Malibu, The Band and Dylan began "rehearsing" songs, obtaining perspective on the thematic and emotional thrusts of Dylan's poetry. Then came the sessions at the Village Recorder (ten of the almost twenty songs recorded there were released on *Planet Waves* in mid-January).

During these months came the Yom Kippur War in Israel, breaking out on 6 October. One member of the United

photographer when Dylan was in Jerusalem in May 1971). The war itself had a deep, immeasurable impact upon all Jews. It was a time, wrote Arnold Sherman, "when God judged and men died." It was both the Sabbath *and* Yom Kippur, the day of awe, of fasting, of prayer. In the Jerusalem streets of Mea Sh'arim, silence reigned with the autumn winds. Then, Egyptian and Syrian MIGs and Sukhois streaked out like steel locusts. "The sound of Jewry's traditional ram's horn," wrote Sherman, "was destined to be eclipsed by the roar of jets. God was signing the obituaries that day." Anti-semitism, a crumbling immoral government, despotic Arab imperialists—these factors (among others) were touching Bob Dylan.

Jewish Appeal sent several letters and telegrams to Dylan, asking for his assistance. He had seen Dylan at the Wailing Wall, sensed Dylan's profound concern with his own soul (reflected in the two photographs which were taken by a UPI

December 1973. The newspaper advertisements had been almost identical, announcing, without photographs or

copy, "Bob Dylan/The Band." The address where orders were to be sent was accompanied by explicit directions as to limitations of tickets and their prices. By noon, Tuesday, 4 December, over 80,000 ticket orders were received at the Forum in Los Angeles. Manager Jim Appell quickly realized that no concert held at the Forum had received such a response. Bill Cunningham, who manages the Oakland Coliseum, was stunned by the 48,000 ticket requests, telling the *San Francisco Examiner* that it was "the greatest response ever for any concert at the Coliseum." The ticket requests did not stop. The Los Angeles Forum would receive over 150,000 and soon it was known that almost six million ticket orders had been sent along the tour's route. In New York alone, almost two million orders virtually overnight flooded Madison Square Garden and the Nassau Veterans Memorial Coliseum in Long Island.

On 7 December, David Geffen announced in Los Angeles that Dylan's holding company, Ashes and Sand, would be Dylan's independent label, to be distributed by Elektra-Asylum. The Dylan/The Band album was first called *Ceremonies of the Horsemen*, then *Love Songs*, finally *Planet Waves*. In San Francisco, at the office of Mr. Graham's FM Productions, the twelve- to fifteen-member road crew was mapping its strategy (by the time the tour was finishing in California, it became obvious that their work was monumental in proportions). Columbia Records released *Dylan*, a powerful collection of renditions: "MR. BOJANGLES," "SARAH JANE," and others. (Many of these songs dated from a 30 March 1970 recording session, which was the basis for a large part of *Self Portrait*.)

Confusion settled in some communities. Concerts scheduled 1 February (University of Dayton, Ohio) and 2 Feb-

Courtesy of Urban Gwerder. London, 1966

was 14 December, but the Michigan winter did not dampen the aura of expectation. On 3 December, the day after tickets had been announced, the University of Dayton cancellation was announced in a small boxed article in the *Cincinnati Post and Times Star*; the automobiles then raced to Ann Arbor. And passes were rare at this time. "Dylan wants the seats reserved for fans," Bill Graham told one California journalist. "He's adamant that the public should have the tickets and not the industry."

Speaking of Dylan's relation to the industry, Mr. Graham added, "I trust him and I presume he trusts me or we would not be working together on this." In New York, John Hammond, vice-president of Columbia Records' department of talent acquisition (a man whose devotion and belief led Columbia to sign Dylan in late 1961), wished Dylan well. Many remembered Dylan's first album, released March 1962, which sold less

ruary (University of Notre Dame) were cancelled. In Ann Arbor, the new site was the University of Michigan's Hill Auditorium, and a long line of people stood in the icy winds waiting for tickets being sold at a tiny box office. It

א	ב	ג	ד	ה	ו	ז	ח	ט
Aleph	Bayt Vayt	Ghimel	Dallet	Hay	Vav or Waw	Zayn	Hhayt	Tayt
1	2	3	4	5	6	7	8	9
י	כ	ל	מ	נ	ס	ע	פ	ע
Yod	Kaf Khaf	Lammed	Mem	Noun	Sammekh	Ayn	Pay Phay	Tsadde
10	20	30	40	50	60	70	80	90
ק	ר	ש	ת	ך	ם	ן	ף	ץ
Qof	Raysh	Seen Sheen	Tav	final Khaf	final Mem	final Noun	final Phay	final Tsadde
100	200	300	400	500	600	700	800	900

than 7,000 copies during its first year. Many called Dylan "Hammond's folly." But, almost twelve years later, the "folly" was a well-read, gentle, perceptive poet.

In Malibu, the atmosphere was brisk and joyous. Dylan was practising each day, alone and with The Band. At the Village Recorder, Rob Fraboni, who engineered *Planet Waves*, was proud of his work on the album and, like everyone else, was thrilled by the tour. "They were so completely professional and together," Fraboni told Eliot Tiegel of *Billboard*, "that once Bob played the song for them, they had the changes down pat." As with the tour, security precautions were high. The November sessions were booked by The Band under the name "Judge Magney" at Studio B. Only a few people attended the three sessions, which usually began at noon and lasted until after nine o'clock at night. David Geffen came by, as did Jackie DeShannon and Cher Bono, but the mainline crew consisted of Dylan, The Band, Mr. Fraboni and assistant engineer Nat Seligman.

Bill Graham: a man quick to smile and equally quick to anger; a man of contradictions, a man of Jewish consciousness. Born Wolfgang Grajonca in Berlin, of Russian-Jewish descent, he lost both parents in the Nazi extermination camps (his mother in Bergen-Belsen). In 1942, he came to the United States, alone and frightened, and was placed into Jewish foster homes by the Jewish Child Care Association of New York. The Holocaust had a "devastating influence" on Bill Graham, according to an individual who has known him since childhood; it forced him to "create an inner world." One sister, now living in San Francisco, was a survivor of several camps and fought in the Hungarian underground. Three other sisters are scattered: one in

Switzerland, one in Austria, and another in San Jose, California. Bill Graham: a ten-year apprenticeship in the rat race of the business world—Alice Chalmers (farming equipment), 3M Corporation, and Southern Pacific. Later, with Howard Stein, he formed the Improvisio Theatre Company, then was active with Ron Davis and the San Francisco-based Mime Troupe. Married, divorced, with one son, David. A driving, energetic man. Yet Bill Graham (for the first time, according to those close to him) was in awe of Bob Dylan, maintaining a respectful distance from the artist, but always there when Dylan needed him.

"We're trying to make this whole thing as uncrazy as possible," David Geffen told John Rockwell of the *New York Times*, a week before the tour began. "But the most significant thing of all about this tour has been the overwhelming response to it." Those who had dismissed Dylan's explorations into his soul were silent, as millions of people ordered tickets to see and hear a poet whom the "critics" had dismissed as "irrelevant." Mr. Graham's two trucks carrying equipment were on their way to Chicago, equipped with extra gasoline tanks. Starship I, like an angry dragonfly, stood waiting in Los Angeles. Dylan, in Malibu, was spending hours talking with his friends, taking time to silently assess what he would see, what he would say.

A little after 3:00 in the afternoon, 2 January, Starship I began to taxi down the runway. There was a one-hour delay—Robbie Robertson arrived late (excited, smiling, nervous), bounding up the metal steps, giving Dylan a brief hug and smile, briefly looking around at the understated opulence of the Boeing 720. The plane is owned by Ward Sylvester (Bobby Sherman's manager), who leases

Dylan at home in Woodstock, New York, 1966.

COURTESY OF URBAN GWERDER

it out for touring groups. For the flights during his tour, Dylan was given specially-prepared organic food, tea and no milk products, according to Lou Weinstock, who works for Toby Roberts Tours of Los Angeles. The jet departed from West Imperial Terminal, a private airport used by others, including Hugh Hefner. Much of the organizational leg-work was done by Barry Imhoff's former secretary, Dilly Dally, who left to work with Mr. Weinstock at Toby Roberts Tours: she tagged the luggage, had the contracts signed. "The energy was high," she said to me in a conversation (20 May 1974). Said Mr. Weinstock of Dylan: "He was very warm, very unpretentious." Dylan on 2 January: quiet, watchful. In the luggage compartment of Starship I were the special guitars he purchased from collector Norman Harris: a 1951 Telecaster, a proto 1953 Stratacaster, and a 1951 D-28 Martin (information courtesy of Robb Lawrence, author of the forthcoming *The Story of American Guitars*).

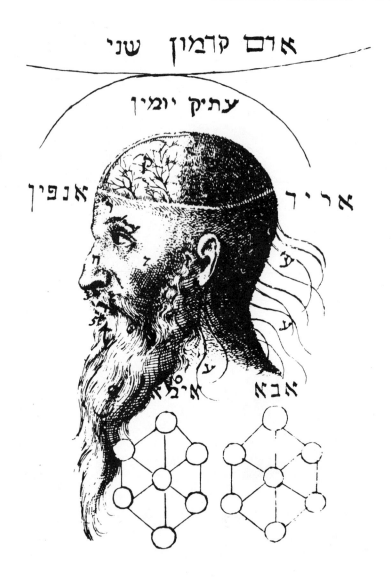

Chicago, Ill.

Chicago

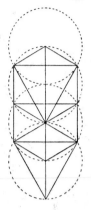

Chicago Stadium, 3 January 1974: neo-classical frescoes on top of building's face. four boxers. five, da Vinci-like shot-putters. discus and javelin. bicycles. discus and javelins. more bicycles. right over gates one and three are wrestlers. fire escapes. snow—powdery, Hawaiian sand. trucks. walking east— "Bob Dylan-The Band"—Chicago in winter, the first day of Tour 74.

7:58: Five Sabbath-like candles are on the stage. For a brief time, Graham and two or three aides were making adjustments (when they had arrived this morning, the cold from the ice under the rubber mats on the stadium's main floor stiffened even the fingers of the piano tuner). The props are pieces of furniture: a bed (blue, bare mattress), a wooden barrel, a brown couch, coat-rack (shaped like a tree). A frisbee is thrown, and a green balloon floated with fragile intensity above the heads in the audience. Not yet is there the *orot lachash*, lights of silence which always prevailed in the earlier 1965–1966 American-European tour; instead, there is an expectation among us. Another balloon (pink) makes an effort to reach up—but it hangs for a moment, then falls again onto the red wooden seats.

By Dylan's microphones is the wooden stand which—outside of his appearances at the Woody Guthrie Memorial, Bangla Desh, Edwardsville, Missouri, and Isle of Wight concerts—always stood by him. More balloons–all colors, one shaped like an udder—extend plastic images into the bright blue cigarette smoke. Within, one can feel spiritual anticipation—the shadows of the *Shekhinah*, of zoharic firmaments in the mind. In the faces of those in my soul, I see the searching eyes of medieval kabbalists and modern searchers: Yitzhak Luria, Avraham Kuk, even Abraham Joshua Heschel. On the stage, latter-day "kabbalists": sound technicians with earphones, aides of Mr. Graham scurrying about. Lights are darkening . . . candles brighter. Lights on amplifiers shine like eyes.

8:28: Dylan is coming up on stage. *Blonde on Blonde*-like scarf. Drinks water from paper cup, resting near acoustic guitar. Electric guitar rips into consciousness. "Yes, the gal I got"— "HERO BLUES" . . . stage in blue lights. Dylan's voice echoing and crying out . . . about the woman with "new movies inside her head" . . .

"LAY, LADY LAY" . . . Dylan's hands (white spider in hall's darkness) leap down his guitar's neck. Dylan's voice is harsher. The Band's mathematics stagger the eyes. "Colors in your *mind*"— words, like images, snapped out . . . poetic bullwhips. Dylan's black suede recalling Spanish outlaw look at Newport Folk Festival 1965 . . . lights flickering, spotlighting notes . . . orange light, red.

"TOUGH MAMA" . . . "I've gained some recognition / But I lost my appetite" . . . Dylan stepping back after each line, then leaning into microphone, his blue eyes touching faces here and there among us . . . "Tough *Mama!*" . . . "I'm gonna go down to the river" . . . Images rushing . . . Mr. Tambourine's "smoke rings" exploding forth . . . "Can I blow a little smoke on you" . . . Levon Helm's face twisted in concentration . . . Richard Manuel watching Dylan watching . . .

Lights fade, then brighten . . . Dylan still playing, standing to one side . . . "THE NIGHT THEY DROVE OLD DIXIE DOWN" . . . Levon's voice conjuring pain and destruction . . . "You can't raise a Caine back up / When he's in defeat" . . . Robbie's guitar a magician's hat . . . 1865 wedded to 1974 . . . our hearts quicken . . .

"STAGE FRIGHT" . . . the "heart of a lonely kid" . . . Rick Danko's soul tearing out its inner depths . . . the "moment of truth" appearing . . . just "never show the fear that's in your eyes" . . .

Dylan steps forth out of dimness . . . his voice slower . . . "IT AIN'T ME, BABE" . . . dualism . . . she is looking for only impossibilities . . . "to open each and ev'ry door" . . . But it's not the poet's task to enslave his heart . . . his voice lingers over each situation, then snaps us back into reality . . .

Dylan steps back . . . Robbie and Rick whisper with him . . . then a crackling electric guitar beginning by Dylan . . .

CHUCK OSGOOD

NEAL PRESTON

"LEOPARD-SKIN PILL-BOX HAT" . . . We go to watch "the sun rise" . . . she in her hat . . . her garage door of the mind standing open . . . Dylan's voice satirical, humorous . . . but seriously painting on his canvas . . . "I *know* what he *really* loves you for" . . .

"It's a heartache" . . . The Band's voices ring out . . . Dylan, again standing in semi-darkness, playing harmonica, his left boot tapping in time . . .

Robbie's guitar pulsates like a metallic vein . . . Dylan adjusts his harmonica holder . . . then, his voice risen high . . . "ALL ALONG THE WATCHTOWER" . . . Isaiah's images blister indifference . . . the Joker, the Thief . . . "too much confusion" . . . Dylan eyes narrowed . . . unsmiling, as his guitar (held to one side like a rifle) embellishes his symbols . . . the watchtower of Zion . . . the Jewish poet leaves no heart untouched . . . "the wind began to howl" . . . Dylan steps back from the microphone, turns

to Robbie . . . the music builds to a crescendo . . . audience is on its feet . . .

The Band begins . . . Dylan a ghost-like shadow as the spotlights illuminate them . . . "she walked out on me" . . . Pain of the words sketching the paralysis of people talking and not talking . . .

Richard, now sitting at his electric piano, rocking forward like an orthodox rabbi . . . "KING HARVEST" . . . his voice subtle, deceptively tranquil . . . corn fields, rice in meadows, blowing winds . . .

Dylan unstraps his guitar, walks silently . . . audience stirs when he puts on his glasses, sits at the piano (Richard has now gone to the second set of drums by Levon), looks up at Rick Danko and Robbie Robertson . . . The piano, like that in a bar-room, tinkles, then deepens . . . the first Halloween notes . . . "BALLAD OF A THIN MAN" . . . brief tidal wave of applause . . . audience is

NEAL PRESTON

NEAL PRESTON

stunned into silence, as Dylan's voice savagely, passionately attacks Mr. Jones . . . "Oh my God / Am I here all alone?" . . . Something is happening to Mr. Jones, who pays for his ticket, and is asked, "How *does* it feel / To be such a *freak*" . . . Dylan's hands rushing over the keyboard—images of transcending Jerry Lee Lewis . . . "You should be *made* / To *wear* a telephone" . . . Dylan, pounding piano, half-standing . . . audience on its feet . . . Dylan turns, then is absorbed into the darkness which surrounds the backstage area . . . Immediately The Band begins . . . Richard moves rapidly back to his piano, and one can see Dylan putting on his electric guitar . . . Levon's drums pound, Robbie's guitar laughs and cries . . . "UP ON CRIPPLE CREEK" . . . "A drunkard's dream" . . .

The air crackles with excitement . . . Dylan adjusting his harmonica holder . . . the first notes of his guitar, and one recognizes "I DON'T BELIEVE YOU" . . . images of 1966 in my mind: Dylan, pale-faced, fragile, would begin with his harmonica, saying, "It used to sound like that, now it sounds like this" . . . Dylan's voice . . . "wild blazing nighttime" . . . "her skirt swayed as the guitar played" (Robbie's guitar wails) . . . Dylan's humor combined with biting realism . . . "Is it easy to for*get*" . . . just find another, pretending "that you *never* have met" . . .

Dylan turns to the audience, smiles quickly, and leans toward the microphone . . . "It'll be about fifteen minutes" . . . lights come on, and the audience is clapping, whistling . . . 9:35 . . .

For this world is like a narrow bridge for man, which he has to pass and there is no danger in the bridge, only fear. But the principle of bracing oneself so that one may pass the bridge in peace, is faith . . . All beginnings are difficult, and especially so, when it comes to Teshu-

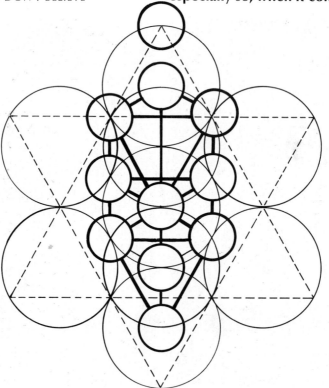

<u>vah</u> (turning). **For it is impossible to be aroused to <u>Teshuvah</u> with sincerity unless the luminosity of His blessed Name begins to spark. It is through the response to the sparking of this light, that a person can be aroused to do <u>Teshuvah</u>. But it is also impossible that this light begin to shine for him unless he does <u>Teshuvah</u> first, for he who is still a stranger and an alien, cannot absorb holiness.**

—Rabbi Nachman of Bratzlav.

Lights dim twice, then darken . . . Dylan comes out on stage, in a white coat . . . picks up his acoustic Martin, adjusts his harmonica holder . . . Then, in a voice that is soft yet harsh, tense yet insistent, begins "THE TIMES THEY ARE A-CHANGIN'" . . . The audience is electrified . . . the 1963 song had been a serious, but humorous challenge, an exclamation point . . . Now the words are *urgent* . . . "the waters around you have grown" . . .

More than "political protest" . . . moral outrage . . . "For the wheel's still in spin" . . . The wheel—the soul—burning with fire, sparks in Dylan's eyes . . . Everyone is aware of Dylan's passionate words . . . his "mystic inner self" (as one friend described it years ago) is repainting old words anew; now we hear strains of *Planet Waves'* intensification . . . "The line it is drawn / The curse it is cast" . . . Dylan leans back, then forward, and his harmonica shrilly, painfully sings, echoing throughout the hall . . . thunderous, extended applause . . . Chooses another harmonica . . .

"SONG TO WOODY" . . . beyond words . . . Dylan's voice soft, almost, then finally cracking with emotion, evocation . . . Woody Guthrie's spirit stalks the aisles . . . the dust bowl seems to swirl in the lights . . . a certain sadness in Dylan's voice, a calling out to a close human being who is gone . . . "Seems sick an' it's hungry, it's tired an' it's torn" . . .

NEAL PRESTON

January 1961, Dylan first played the song for Woody himself . . . Dylan steps back from the microphone, his blue eyes almost misty (the bright lights? the energies of the song?), his guitar sounding distant, like a train in Montana late at night . . .

Changes harmonicas . . . begins strumming the Martin even before it can be heard over the microphones . . . Turns to audience, a lilting harmonica introduction of a few notes . . . Then . . . "THE LONESOME DEATH OF HATTIE CARROLL" . . . the horror of brutalizing death, both physical and spiritual . . . the bigotry . . . "high office relations in the politics of Maryland" . . . William Zanzinger (when the song was first published, it was Zantzinger), killer with a cane at a dinner party . . . Hattie Carroll, fifty-one years old, ten children . . . The judge, the legal foundation, giving Zanzinger six months for "penalty and repentance" . . . Dylan's sarcasm so evident . . .

Spotlights shift . . . Dylan's eyes look questioningly at the thousands of faces as he begins guitar intricacies . . . "NOBODY BUT YOU" . . . Nothing "reaches me, except you" . . . "I feel I'm on fire . . . Nothin 'round here I care to try for, except you / Nothing 'round here I care to die for, except you" . . . His voice singing rapidly, the images rising then settling in our minds . . . "I'm a stranger here / And no one sees me" . . . the "water from the well" is gone . . . The harmonica sounds like the inner voice of forgotten hymns, chants, Yiddish parables . . . The audience silent for a moment, then the applause is deafening . . . Dylan immediately begins another song, holding his guitar up to the microphones . . .

"IT'S ALRIGHT, MA" . . . mysticism . . . reality . . . false gods . . . affirmation of life . . . We all have to stand naked sometimes . . . Dylan's voice pleading, angry, insisting . . . "temptation's page" . . .

"waterfalls of pity" . . . How people have been used as investments . . . "as human gods aim for their mark" . . . "But it's alright, Ma, it's life, and life *only*" . . .

Audience on its feet . . . Dylan bows . . . nods to those in the balconies sitting behind the stage . . . Thousands of matches and lighters illuminating the stadium . . . Dylan has been gone almost ten minutes, but his presence looms in our hearts . . . A girl near me is openly crying . . . A young Hasidic Jew, with flowing ear-locks and round black hat, is laughing and smiling, nodding to me, raising a clenched fist . . . The applause building in torrents, like rain tapping, then pounding on a tin roof . . . the matches and lighters still flickering . . . Spotlights now illuminating the backstage area . . . The Band coming back on stage . . .

Poetry is a choosing in the infinite; and this choosing is not a hunting, seeking, a sifting, rather, it is a fire that has extinguishing and dissolving force. Each word of the poet is single; and yet there lies around each a ring of ungraspable material which represents the sphere of infinite vanishing; that is the track of the dissolving force of fire . . . Of the poet it can be said that his heart is the hub into which the spokes of polarities converge: here is not a suspension, however, but union, not indifference but fruitfulness. The poet bears the antitheses of the spirit, and in him they are fruitful.
—Martin Buber, <u>Daniel:</u>
<u>Dialogues on Realization.</u>

Dylan coming back up on stage . . . thunderous, wild applause . . . He quickly straps on his electric guitar, turns to Robbie adjusting his harmonica holder . . . then turns to microphone . . . "FOREVER YOUNG" . . . "May you build a ladder to stars / Climb on every rung"—Jacob's ladder, the ladder of a later time ("I saw a white ladder all covered with water": "A HARD RAIN'S A-GONNA FALL") . . . "May you *stay* forever *young*" . . . Dylan's voice caressing his words . . . "May you have a strong foundation . . . your song always be sung" . . . his harmonica stressing the miracle of love between father and children, those intangibilities beyond words . . .

Retuning his guitar, Dylan turns his back on the audience . . . turns again to microphone . . . "SOMETHING THERE IS ABOUT YOU" . . . love that "lights a match in me" . . . Dylan singing hard . . . a cry against confusion which only distracts the heart and the soul . . .

Dylan turns, changes harmonicas . . . a whispered conference with Robbie, Rick, and Levon . . . Robbie smiles . . . begins a few notes . . . Dylan takes lead . . . the drums and organ blend together . . . Then . . . "*Once* upon a time" . . . audience going wild, on its feet, clapping, cheering . . . "LIKE A ROLLING STONE" . . . Dylan simultaneously teasing and venomous . . . Memories flood the mind . . . remembering Newport and Forest Hills and Berkeley Community Theater in 1965 . . . "You *used* to laugh about" . . . We suddenly see the politics of relationship, of experience . . . remembering . . . "How *does* it *feel?*" . . . Everyone singing the chorus back to Dylan . . . "You *never* turned around to *see* the *frowns* on the jugglers and the clowns" . . . His eyes bright, Dylan pouring everything out . . . "Napolean in *rags* and the language that he *used*" . . .

11:00: Everyone standing . . . Dylan disappears into the darkness . . . the candles on the stage jump in the moving air . . . Waves and waves of passionate calling for Dylan to return . . . five minutes . . . seven minutes pass by . . . Then . . . Dylan's returning! . . . The Band quickly go to their instruments . . . Dylan standing to one side, playing his harmonica . . . "THE WEIGHT" . . . The Band transcending chaos . . . arriving in Nazareth . . . "I just need some place where I can lay my head" . . . Taking loads away . . . "you put the load right on me" . . . Dylan tapping his boot in time, blowing into his harmonica which echoes throughout . . . Audience still on its feet . . . Dylan puts his harmonica back into his shiny metal holder . . . turns to his microphones . . .

An explosion of sight and sound . . . "MOST LIKELY YOU GO YOUR WAY" . . . "I'm just gonna let you *pass*" . . . Dualism . . . chaos, peace, love, contempt . . . blonde on blonde . . . the Jewish soul assailing obsequiousness . . . "It *can't* be this way *every*-where" . . . Dylan bending notes, bouncing about behind the microphones, leaning over the microphone . . . "Time will *tell* just who fell / And who's been left *behind*" . . .

Everyone standing, clapping, cheering . . . Dylan steps back, departs with a small bow . . . Five minutes pass . . . Smiles, the rumble of departing people high in the balconies, everyone talking at once . . .

Maureen Orth—formerly of the *Village Voice*, now of *Newsweek*—would be able, after the first night's concert, to sit with Dylan for a few moments. He was excited, yet cautious. "There's a new generation of people now, a new time," he told Ms. Orth. "My father had to sweat. My father lived in a lot of pain. In this earthly body he didn't transcend the pain, the pain of material things . . . The '60s were filled with it (war and spiritual unrest). It has helped me to grow up. The '70s are more realistic, but the '60s exposed the roots of that realism."

A few miles from Dylan's hotel are other "Jews"—some of whom came to tonight's concert. As in New York, many

of them wear rings through their noses, sing Baptist hymns, and wear skullcaps. Some claim to be B'nai Zaken, sons of ancient Israelites. They call other Jews Edomites, insisting that Abraham, Isaac, and Jacob, like them, were black. Their synagogue is on South Carpenter Street, in Chicago's surreal black district; in their daily services, heavily-accented Hebrew is supplemented with "that's right" and "Ay-men." A storm rages over what one sees here—matching in intensity, if not in scale, Dylan's public prayer/poetry.

Rabbi Ahzrael Devine has never attended an orthodox yeshiva, nor has he been ordained, nor has he followed Jewish law and converted. Yet he, and his followers, claim to be Jews. Chicago's black Jews have been claiming their rights since 1925, but only recently, when several went to Israel, have they encountered Jewish law. Some converted under tutelage of Israel's orthodox rabbis, others refused, claiming Israeli rabbis are "violating" Torah.

"People are willing to fight for white Jewry all over the world, but not for black Jewry," Devine stated to one reporter. "If only they would realize that Israel today is like Joseph's coat of many colors."

A young black Jew stands, chanting. I sway, allowing the words their solace in my soul, the *t'fillin* binding me to the *Shem*, the Name.

CHUCK OSGOOD

The evening of the second Chicago concert, 4 January: Tonight the Sabbath—man prepares his soul for twenty-four hours of invocation of the inner light. If wishes were horses, says an old Yiddish proverb, beggars would ride. We are adjacent to infinity—if one laughs, the heavens laugh; if one cries, the heavens share the sorrow. On the Sabbath we strive for *menucha*, for inner still-

ness, so that we can walk "beside the still waters" (Psalm 23:2), which are, said the ancient Rabbis, of the eternal within. Facing tempestuousness, our soul becomes tired, needing *tikkun*, reintegration. We receive, we greet the Sabbath. Wrote Rabbi Abraham Joshua Heschel, of blessed memory: "We must conquer space in order to sanctify time. All week long we are called upon to sanctify life through employing things of space. On the Sabbath it is given to us to share in the holiness that is in the heart of time."

Menahem-Mendl of Vitebsk, the disciple of the nineteenth-century Hasidic rabbi, the Maggid of Mezeritch, once said: "My mission on earth is to recognize the voice—inside and outside me —and fill it." He also said: "Man is the language of God." *Veda ma lemala mimkha*: know that which occurs up above, derives from you as well.

It has been told of Zusia and Elimelekh, eighteenth-century Hasidim and pious brothers, that wherever they stayed, the place became a part of the Hasidic world. Except a small village in Poland, which caused restlessness. The village was Auschwitz.

7:30: On the main floor, the edge of

the stage is about 130 feet away. The hat-rack stands, statuesque, forlorn with no hats. Dylan's three acoustic Martins and his Epiphone electric rest, like lyres, in their stands . . . A blue child's balloon listlessly rests in the air, held by invisible hands—then suddenly falls. A young girl nervously taps two sticks of unlit incense against the back of the chair in front of her. What are her thoughts, her dreams, her sorrows? She may have seen John Prine here last night. She may have seen herself . . . Rimbaud once said that, even if the poet goes mad after having seen his visions, at least he lived afterwards.

8:20: Bill Graham comes out to the microphone—"I would ask that you refrain from smoking." Mixed cheers. "No tape recorders please. If you've got flash cameras, please don't use them." A flash camera goes off. "If you've got regular cameras, shoot all you want, but only from your seating area." Anticipation is growing . . . Candles are lit . . .

8:30: Lights beginning to darken . . . Dylan appears with The Band . . . roars of welcome . . . The Band quickly putting themselves into position . . . Dylan nervous (black coat, brown boots, black jeans, white shirt-tail out) . . . Back to audience, as he straps on his Epiphone . . . Turns, guitar held to his side, his eyes glinting in the bright lights . . . "IT AIN'T ME, BABE" . . . evocation of David—Martin Buber's *Daniel*—the rungs of consciousness . . . The precision of The Band—their love of spiritual tonality is moving . . . "gather flowers *constantly*" . . . Deserted dreams, betrayed trust . . . Do fishermen still hold flowers on Desolation Row?

The essence of the Jewish spirit . . . consists in rejecting despair. It consists in admitting that yes, society is not without evil; yes, we do have enemies, and they are powerful; yes, they do want our

NEAL PRESTON

destruction. But so what! We still cannot allow ourselves to despair . . . Alone, the individual Jew would have been lost many times and long ago, but a Jew is never alone. Being Jewish is a remedy against solitude, for a Jew is forever surrounded by his community, visible or invisible. Jews have never before been so oganically linked to one another. If we shout here, we are being heard in Kiev. If Jews cry in Kiev they are heard and worried over in Jerusalem. And if Jews are sad in Jerusalem we are moved to tears here. Thus, a Jew lives in more than one place in more than one time. A Jew lives on more than one level and he lives more than one life.

— Elie Wiesel, 1973.

Audience exploding . . . A single spotlight illuminates Dylan as he walks on stage, Martin guitar throbbing against the movements of his white coat . . . "THE TIMES THEY ARE A-CHANGIN' " . . . Not a sound for a battle charge, but a passionate announcement of pathos, of our participation in evolution . . . "come writers and cri-*tics*" . . .

"LOVE MINUS ZERO/NO LIMIT" . . . Dylan moving his voice into incantation . . . "ceremonies of the horsemen" . . . revolution/turning/returning . . . beginning in the soul . . .

Here are some reasons not to despair. Our Israel is still here. Jewish solidarity is stronger than ever and purer than ever. Diaspora Jews have shown a heightened awareness of their kinship with the people of Israel. . . . The Jews who went through the Holocaust are the strongest Jews on earth. Oh, are they vulnerable! But nothing can crush them. They have already gone through everything it is possible to go through. From the strength they have earned from despair, these Jews have drawn new

hope. Despair should be, must be overcome. Despair can be transmuted; it can become a tremendous power. From this power, this despair, a Jew can draw new hope.

— Elie Wiesel, 1973.

10:35: Dylan walks out on stage . . . shouts for "Rolling Stone! Rolling Stone!" . . . Robbie sets his electric guitar down, picks up an acoustic . . . Dylan begins . . . Levon's mandolin in background . . . "FOREVER YOUNG" . . . ladder of Jacob's dreams . . . Dylan, looking like a yeshiva student—full of promise, defender of hope . . . like the Psalmist: "may your *song* always be sung" . . .

10:55: Together, quickly, they depart the stage . . . Chicago Stadium a moving sea of happiness . . . people reaching out with their souls . . . five minutes . . . They are returning! . . . Dylan, a long gray scarf hanging about his neck . . . He smiles . . . everyone clapping in time . . . "I *ain't* gonna work on Maggie's Farm *no* more!" . . . More images—Newport 1965—Dylan, in leather jacket, singing the same song with the same biting challenge . . . "*Every*body wants you / To be just like *them*" . . .

Dylan bows . . . Levon raises a fist . . . Shouts: "more! more!" . . . A vacuum— where there had been communication— being quickly filled with departure . . .

He grounds all duality in unity. But out of each work polarity arises for him anew: renewed. Rejuvenated, sharpened, deepened, it summons him to new deeds. Thus the poet is the messenger of God and of the earth and is at home in the two spheres. The force of fire is his force; it burns in contradiction, and it shines in unity. Like Enoch, of whom a legend tells that he was transformed from flesh to fire; his bones are glowing coals, but his eyelashes are the splendor of the firmament.

—Martin Buber, <u>Daniel:</u>
<u>Dialogues on Realization.</u>

It is still the Sabbath. The chants of an old Polish rabbi can be heard through snow and winds. Wrote the Sassover Rebbe, Moses Leib, who died in 1807, may his name and memory be blessed: "The Sabbath should be the 'Delight of Our Hearts.' If, however, it has become a Sad Day, it is surely because of our uncleanness on the days of the week. It is like a man who comes out of a dark place and cannot endure the light."

The tender roots of the sycamore tree split the rocky crags. Man/woman reaches forth, touching leaves, allowing the sap to run like water. He/she raises a voice, and the echoes loosen distant sand.

Song, Hasidism taught, is a ladder, whereby man comes to a heightened consciousness. **It has many rungs and must descend into dark depths before it can rise to luminous heights. It unites what is above with what is below and evokes forms yet unseen. Great is the the song composed of words and melodies, greater is the song in which melody suffices, but greatest is the song that needs neither words nor music.**
—Ruth Mintz.

Dylan, resting in his hotel room after the second concert in Chicago, talked to a few journalists, and looked over press reactions to his first concert. Most of these were glowing, but lacked a grasp of something beyond type on paper: the poet's foundations. Dylan, in the liner notes for *Bringing It All Back Home*, had written of former people (Mozart, Bach, and others): "They are all dead." The Jewish poet embraces life.

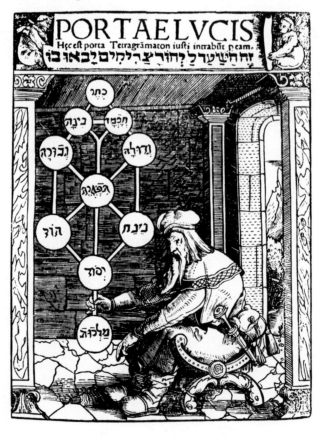

Philadelphia, Pa.

Philadelphia, Pa.

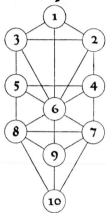

When necessary—with what Rabbi Heschel, of blessed memory, calls a "passion for sincerity"—Bob Dylan creates sparks where before were only the signature of thoughts: auroras, theosophic compasses, laughter, trains which cause the waters of wells to transform themselves into tears. We give birth to ladders of light, rungs of the silence between words heard at Sinai, held tightly in guitar strings and the incantations of a harmonica. Knocking on heaven's door, lamenting on the gates of Eden, man remembers the oaths of a Hattie Carroll. Last night, matches held aloft in the Chicago Stadium joined five candles on the stage; last night was the Sabbath and the poet's words became conversation with the *Shekhinah*, as the candles seemed to become eyes. For a brief moment, the poet inhaled the promises of Johanna, and exhaled his promises to his soul.

We desire release. Do we not grasp, like Bob Dylan, for hope, for love? We listen to the blowing of the wind, the crackling of the cold leaves in the soul, creating autumn's splendors in our wintry existence. We stand, mountains in the palms of our hands, "rivers that ran through every day" ("I THREW IT ALL AWAY"), on the edges of Highway 61, far from the trees of Eden. "Clear ye in the wilderness . . . a highway for our God" (Isaiah 40:3). The Father of Night creating thematic intonations of the poet's promises to himself, who "fainteth not" and is never "weary" (Isaiah 40:28). The ubiquity of existence is not necessarily equivocal. *Tanya*: it is taught. *Tanya, tanya.* The soft sounds of a word carving initials into existence, into a life which opposes the man teaching himself to pray. Zophar the Na'amathite asks Job: "Canst thou find out the deep things of God? Canst thou attain unto the purpose of the Almighty?" (Job 11:7). We open eyes, seeing the dimensions of the Mystery. Can we expect the finite to make the infinite finite? "And though man be risen up to pursue thee, and to seek thy soul, yet the soul of my lord shall be bound in the bundle of life with the Lord thy God" (First Samuel 25:29).

Bob Dylan, in 1967, wrote of the joys to be found "Underneath That Apple Suckling Tree." Songs, taught one Hasidic rabbi, "are derived from a source of sanctity, from the Temple of Song." We try, Dylan has said, "to harmonize with

white cloth to an aide to continue. The crowds are moving quietly.

The Spectrum (which opened in 1967) is large but comfortable, oval-shaped, with red cushioned chairs. It is not too crowded (even at 8:00 P.M. Overhead, a multi-colored spotlight is tested against a ceiling; so bright, one could easily mistake it for sunlight . . .

8:36: Lights darken and blue spotlights are shining . . . Dylan, guitar in hand . . . red spotlights . . . The Band tuning . . . much quieter . . . Then deafening applause with the first notes . . . "RAINY DAY WOMEN" . . . cheers, shouts . . . "I feel so *all* alone" . . . Harmonics of memory and presentness . . . Dylan wearing sports coat, gray shirt with white, straight collar, dark jeans and brown boots . . . "when you sit down in your grave" . . . Robbie's eyes closed as if in a dream . . . *"Everybody must get stoned!"*

"JUST LIKE TOM THUMB'S BLUES" . . . the

recognition of pain, the possibility of hope, of salvation . . . "picking up Angel" . . ."*just* like a ghost" . . . Audience is ecstatic . . . Dylan leaning over, choosing songs from a long list lying on his stool . . . "IT AIN'T ME, BABE" . . . lyrical harshness, the realization of the necessity of freedom, of release . . .

"I DON'T BELIEVE YOU" . . . the beginning—reminiscent of (yet transcending) the European 1966 tour . . . "something has *changed*" . . . The organ lingers over emotions . . . "Pretend that we *never* have touched" . . . Dylan turns, sets down his guitar, walks to piano . . . "BALLAD OF A THIN MAN" . . . Dylan testing the piano, then quickly the notes grow cohesive, the Halloween-like atmosphere commences for Mr. Jones . . . "When you get *home*" . . . Dislocation of identities, the soul's confusion . . . the illusions of F. Scott Fitzgerald, another casualty . . . Attacking of the imagination . . . "there oughta be a law against you comin' around" . . . Dylan, bent over piano, the blue spotlight playing tricks as Robbie and Rick stand, watching Dylan's fingers leaping over the keyboard . . .

The Lord said to Cain, "Where is Abel your brother?"
And he said, "I do not know; am I my brother's keeper?"
> **One law shall be for the native born**
> **And for the stranger who dwells among you.**
The stranger you shall not oppress.
You indeed have known the soul of the stranger,
For you were strangers in the land of Egypt.
> **You shall love the stranger,**
> **For you were strangers in the land of Egypt.**
The stranger who dwells among you
Shall be as the native born among you.
> **You shall love him as yourself,**

**For you were strangers in the land
of Egypt.
I am the Lord your God.
These are the things that you shall do:
Speak everyone the truth with his
neighbor,
Execute judgment of truth and
peace in your gates,
And let none of you devise evil in
your heart
Against his neighbor.
If your brother becomes poor
And cannot maintain himself with you,
you must support him;
As a stranger and a sojourner he shall
live with you.**
—from the <u>Tanach.</u>

9:55: House lights flickering like
lightning storms . . . The power that is
still present reflects in the comments
and hurried conversation of the audience. One person leans over my
shoulder: "He still has the quality of
looking at life, you know, like Carlos
Castaneda's magician-realist, Don
Juan" . . . 10:00 . . . lights darkening . . .
"Come gather 'round people" . . . Everyone shouting in recognition, the roar
rushing out toward Dylan . . . "THE TIMES
THEY ARE A-CHANGIN' " . . . "battle
outside . . . rattle your walls" . . . Dylan's
voice soaring . . . The joyous announcement of the song is somehow gone, the
rage in him surprising (Michael McClure
is here: his face changing like a cine-
matic screen with each new image) . . .
Song ending . . . everyone on their
feet—*giving* to him . . . "Thank you" . . .
the voice almost engulfed . . .

In almost a whisper Dylan begins . . .
"I'm out here a thousand miles" . . .
"SONG TO WOODY" . . . recognizable
tenderness . . . "I wrote *you* a song" . . .
ghosts of Leadbelly and Cisco float before the consciousness . . . The wind
comes, the dust carries them away . . .

the soul, hard travelling . . . Dylan stepping back from microphone . . . "Turn
around!" someone behind him in the
balcony shouts . . . Dylan smiles, turns
. . . turns to floor audience—a deep,
Charles Chaplin-like bow . . . his fingers
dance across the low-gauge steel strings
. . . a tinkling sound in the notes . . . "MR.
TAMBOURINE MAN" . . . Dylan ends, is
changing guitars, a long standing ovation now . . . the Spectrum thundering
louder after each poem . . .

In 1965, when asked by a friend how
he felt on the subject of death,
Dylan replied that he could "very
easily accept it." Believing, he emphasized, was likewise a "dangerous
business"; that, existentially, one could
not moralize eternity. The roots of his
newer (1965) songs, he also said, were
to be found in "everything"; they were in
"perfect form, where they're supposed
to be," with no disguises, no manufac-
turedness. "I can't save their souls," Dylan said of those reaching into his mind
for salvation. "Tomorrow never comes.
There is no yesterday." There is only the
present.

"Back then," he said of his 1962–1964
songs, "I was me; now I'm *me*." The
newer songs, he said, were "windows."
We lean forward, look through the curtains—seeing reality and not images
(which, he insisted, are those things one
has not seen).

In September of 1965, in Los Angeles,
Dylan spoke to one fan, Paul J. Rob-
bins, of his reality. "It's that nobody
can learn by somebody else showing
them or teaching them. People got to
learn by themselves, going through something which *relates*." Relating—a Buberian act, a human definition. A few days
after his 27 August 1965 concert at Forest
Hills (which saw objects thrown at Dylan
when he launched into "I DON'T BELIEVE
YOU," with electrical backing), Dylan

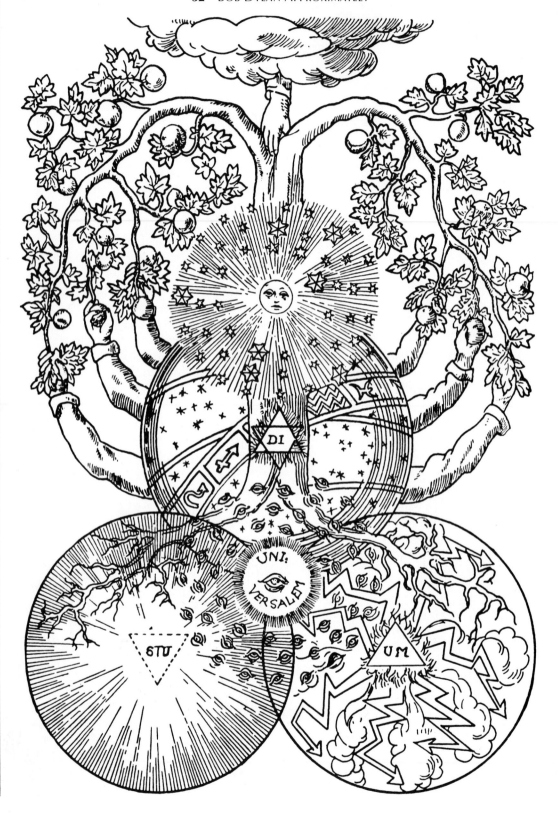

told Robert Shelton of the *New York Times*: "It's all music, no more, no less. I know in my own mind what I'm doing. If anyone has imagination, he'll know what I'm doing. If they can't understand my songs, they're missing something. If they can't understand green clocks, wet chairs, purple lamps or hostile statues, they're missing something, too . . . What I write is much more concise now than before. It's not deceiving."

. . . And praised. Auschwitz. Be. Maidanek. The Lord. Treblinka. And praised. Buchenwald. Be. Mauthausen. The Lord. Belzec. And praised. Sobidor. Be. Chelmno. The Lord. Ponary. And praised. Theresienstadt. Be. Warsaw. The Lord. Vilna. And praised. Skarzysko. Be. Bergen-Belsen. The Lord. Janow. And praised. Dora. Be. Neuengamme. The Lord. Pustkow. And praised. . .
> **—from The Last of the Just by**
> **Andre Schwartz-Bart.**

"KNOCKIN' ON HEAVEN'S DOOR" . . . a frantic, mournful plea . . . The gun, the darkness, man being lost, eclipsed . . . "wipe the blood from my face . . . it's hard to trace" . . . "long black train" . . . Dylan ends song on "Mama, take this badge offa me"—his voice low, harsh . . . stepping back . . .

Freedom includes an act of choice, but its root is in the realization that the self is no sovereign, in the discontent with the tyranny of the ego. Freedom comes about in the moment of transcending the self, thus rising above the habit of regarding the self as its own end. Freedom is an act of self-engagement of the spirit, a spiritual event.
> **—Rabbi Abraham Joshua**
> **Heschel, Man Is Not Alone:**
> **A Philosophy of Religion.**

"WEDDING SONG" . . . Of all versions through the tour, this particular night saw its fullest, most powerful presentation, surpassing even the *Planet Waves* rendition . . . "I love you more than dreams upon the sea" . . . "courtyard of the jester" . . . My hands are shaking, my eyes are rivetted to Dylan . . . He bends forward, pounding the guitar, conjuring every possible variation of emotion for each verse . . . A woman near me has tears streaming down her face . . . "you taught me how to *give*" . . . "quenched my *thirst* and satisfied the *burning* in my *soul*" . . . What is lost is lost . . . we play our song, our inner hymns . . . (note to myself: "Dylan has transcended 'VISIONS OF JOHANNA' and 'SAD-EYED LADY OF THE LOWLANDS'; an ethological articulation of his Jewishness") . . . "*if* there is *eternity* / I'll *love* you there *again*" . . . "love that doesn't cease . . . the past is *gone*" (Dylan screaming out—jarringly) . . . abruptly, as if a tornado has passed, Dylan is stepping back from the microphone, his face determined and eyes staring nowhere; the spell has been cast . . .

"FOREVER YOUNG" . . . psalmic pleading, hoping . . . "may you see the lights surrounding you" . . . Words to the present, the Presence, children . . . we turn

BOB GRUEN

from the hard rain, serving our "strong foundations" . . . our hearts always "joyful" (note to myself: "Serve the Lord with gladness; come before His presence with singing," Psalm 100:2) . . . Dylan's harmonica creating . . .

10:55: "Until we meet again, I'll leave you with these words" . . . Dylan turning back to Robbie, playing a slow lead . . . "Once upon a time" . . . "LIKE A ROLLING STONE" . . . House lights on . . . everyone standing . . . clapping . . . Dylan shouting out words . . . audience singing back . . . *"How does it feel?"* . . . We've all been out on the street . . . "You said you'd *never* compromise with the mystery tramp" . . . Dylan smiles as we sing along . . . he flashes a V-sign. "It was great" . . . the lights hot and bright . . . Dylan walks off stage . . . on his stool remain a few flowers, his harmonica holder, two paper cups . . . smiling . . . waves and waves of applause, cheering . . . He wipes his face with a towel . . . smiles at the audience crowded at the bottom of the tall, stately stage . . .

Said Goethe to his biographer, Eckermann, during one of their first encounters: "It is not good that you pass through here so quickly. I would like to see more of you and speak to you more." Silence has fallen over the Spectrum, and Mr. Graham's equipment crews have started loading the two trucks for the trek to Toronto. The security guards are walking about in protean confusion, unable, it would seem, to understand that what happened earlier was—a concert . . . but more than a combination of thaumaturgical guitars and poetries celebrating Mnemosynism.

The final concert in Philadelphia (7 January) had *moments* of magic duplicated throughout the tour; but, for reasons beyond my verbal capacity, it was probably one of the finest *complete*

concerts, a fusion of Dylan's Jewish passion and The Band's bacchanalian intensity. Sitting in his room at the Sheraton, Dylan spoke briefly to John Rockwell of the *New York Times*: "Now that it's happened, it pleases me. But if it hadn't happened, it wouldn't have disappointed me either. Being on tour is like being in limbo. It's like going from nowhere to nowhere. But at least the audiences are different. The audiences on this tour have been very warm." Regarding *Planet Waves*, Dylan spoke of "SOMETHING THERE IS ABOUT YOU": "It completes a circle for me, about certain things running through my pattern."

The pattern, to be sure, could be ascertained in Dylan's poetry since 1967: beginning with the Dwarf Music demonstration tapes ("I SHALL BE RELEASED," "I'M NOT THERE," "UNDERNEATH THAT APPLE SUCKLING TREE," and others) and including *Planet Waves*. As Richard Rocklin, his rabbi friend of Charlotte, North Carolina, later agreed, Dylan had never lost his Jewishness. Throughout his published writings, Dylan sought avenues of spiritual expression, and following his July 1966 motorcycle accident, he continued examining his Jewish soul.

In Philadelphia, Dylan sought some relaxation. He would go ice-skating in the cold confines of the city, sit and talk with friends (and with his mother and step-father), or spend time by himself. He talked to a few journalists. To *Time* correspondent David DeVoss, Dylan said: "When I first took my music on the road back in '60, it was in search of something else that wasn't being covered. I let it happen by itself, and it grew and matured by itself. Everybody has matured, musicians included. A lot of these people (his admirers) and myself have a great deal in common. As for the music: I just let the rope out."

בס"ד

Toronto, Ont.
Montreal, Que.

Toronto/Montreal

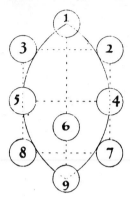

Know that one who knows how to make songs (which means to collect the tiny points of goodness which are found in each and every Jew, even a sinner), is the one who should pray at the head of the congregation. He is called the representative of the congregation, and is designated by them to collect all of the points of goodness found in each one who prays, and all of the points of goodness are collected together in him. And he stands and prays with the goodness in him. And because he exists on a high plane, all of the notes of song (nekudot) are desirous for him. and are gathered together in him. One who knows how to make songs is one who knows how to judge every man by the scale of merit, even the foolish and the wicked; for he seeks as hard as he can to find in them fine points of goodness, like the notes of song. And, by this means, songs are made.

> —Rabbi Nachman of Bratzlav, Liqqutei Moharan (loosely translated by Joel Rosenberg).

The feverish energies of Philadelphia are transposed and rejuvenated in Toronto; the selection of songs (with only a few variations and omissions) sustaining Dylan's studious efforts to show spiritual continuity. Michael McClure is again present, his face alternately sad, frightened, or joyous. Also present is Marshall McLuhan, manipulator of semantic canvas. To the San Francisco poet, McLuhan said, "Violence is the result of loss of identity—the more loss the greater the violence . . . Gravity is like acoustic space—the center is everywhere." Gravity, center, identity, violence—spotlighted, sometimes looking fragile with acoustic guitar and harmonica in the harshness of a Canadian winter, Dylan juggles images and emotions.

"If we learn to sense the Divine center within ourselves," writes Rabbi Burt Jacobson (in an unpublished book, *Lights of the Kabbalah: Spiritual Teachings of Rav Kuk*), "we can gradually integrate the spheres of our consciousness and identity within a totality, and come to see each of our spheres of reality as interpenetrating parts of our Selves, as well as the cosmic organism. In this way we may become instrumental not only in fostering our own personal integration, but in turning all reality back toward its Maker and Master." Turning

reality, all reality, back—becoming mirrors, living reflections, we blow upon the sparks within ourselves and nurture a soul on fire.

To Ben Fong-Torres of *Rolling Stone*, Dylan said: "For me, (Dylan's political songs) were just reinforcing those images in my head that were there, that don't die, that will be there tomorrow. And in doing so for myself, hopefully also for those people who also had those images . . . Sure, there's still a message. But the same electric spark that went off back then could still go off again—the spark that led to nothing. Our kids will probably protest, too. Protest is an old thing. Sometimes protest is deeper, or different—the Haymarket Riot, the Russian Revolution, the Civil War—that's protest. There's always a need for protest songs. You just gotta tap it."

In Toronto, The Band—perhaps remembering their old gruelling bar circuit with Ronnie Hawkins—seemed to present their songs with new fervor. After their evening concert, 9 January, Dylan and The Band slipped away and went to Toronto's Nickelodeon, of which Hawkins is half-owner. They were accompanied by Ms. Roberta Richards, manager

PHOTOS BY ART USHERSON

of Leon Redbone, in whom Dylan has maintained a high interest.

Hawkins had wanted to play with Dylan and The Band privately, but members of the audience were too intrusive. So Dylan, The Band, Hawkins, Bill Graham, and others went back to Inn On The Park where Dylan stayed at a modest, comfortable, $120-a-day room, drinking herbal tea, playing chess with Lou Kemp as Garth Hudson and Hawkins sang along to *Planet Waves*. After Dylan's return to his hotel, he departed again (at nearly 2:00 A.M.), and a sleepy Joseph Sia (one of contemporary music's most talented photographers) was awakened in the living room of his friend Gordon Lightfoot. At first, Sia thought he was dreaming—but no; Dylan, Rick Danko, and Gordon Lightfoot stood in the dimness of the room, talking. Dylan was warm and relaxed, a little tired.

Time don't exist, it's an illusion, the other side of Dali's clocks . . . Know where God is? The river, that's God. The river's right where you're standing, and it's up in the mountains, and it's down the bend, and into the sea. All at the same instant. If there's a God, the river's Him.
—Dylan, 1964.

The Ba'al Shem Tov, the founder of Hasidism, said of silence and solitude: In singing our inner hymns, we should endeavor to do so in a quiet voice, "but with all the strength in us. . . . Any cry unto the Lord from a heart at one with Him should be in silence, as we read: 'Their heart cried unto the Lord' (Lamentations 2:18)."

Bob Dylan—laughing and smiling on the stages in both Toronto and Montreal . . . the spotlights playing with shadows. Dylan—creating images and hymns.

When he read Martin Buber after his motorcycle accident, one wonders if he read Buber's famous anthologies of Hasidic stories, in particular, a story of Rabbi Pinhas of Koretz, of blessed memory (died 1791). Rabbi Pinhas said, "When a man is singing and cannot lift his voice, and another comes and sings with him, another who can lift his voice, then the first will be able to lift his voice too. That is the secret of the bond between spirit and spirit."

The limitations of language: we see the child (the daughter, the son, the brother, the sister) and know not what to say. We see a star falling over the skies of

Montreal (11 January), a pigeon searching for food in the frozen avenues outside the Montreal Forum. Words become symbols, useful when heard, moving mountains when spoken.

"Be not rash with thy mouth," it is taught, "and let not thy heart be hasty to utter a word before God; for God is in heaven, and thou upon earth; therefore let thy words be few" (Lamentations 5:1). Few words, not total silence.

We knock at heaven's door. We open our own doors "to the roadside" (Job 31:32), touching the hands of strangers and orphans. We drive "all memory and fate . . . deep beneath the waves" ("MR. TAMBOURINE MAN") of the river of life; facing the morning, the noon, and the evening with the promise of love and loves. The judgments of God, it is said, are "like the great deep" (Psalm 36:7), far beneath the waves of concrete. We cannot find wisdom or love in darkness, Bob Dylan has been saying since *John Wesley Harding*. "The deep saith: 'It is not in me'; And the sea saith: 'It is not with me' " (Job 28:14). "As the mountains press down the deep," says one rabbinic commentary, "that it may not rise and flood the world, so righteous deeds press iniquities down."

We see the supreme Thought, the Thought which embraces all things, the Thought which contains the power and fullness of the Whole. We see that all the great rivers flow from it, and streams issue from the rivers, and brooks from the streams, and the brooks divide into many channels, and the channels divide into many thousands, indeed an infinity of little canals, which pour forth the bounty of will, life, and thought.

—Rabbi Avraham Yitzhak Kuk (trans. J. Agus).

Boston, Mass.

Boston

אין סוף
כתר
חכמה
בינה
גדולה
גבורה
תפארת
נצח
הוד
יסוד
מלכות

Cold, snow and ice-lined streets. A record store has, in its front window, a green sign with yellow lettering, announcing Dylan and The Band's appearance tonight. The eyes linger on a tall statue of a Revolutionary War Minuteman on Battle Green, in the center of Lexington. Battle Green—the site of the first fighting for the revolutionary ideas of a young, contradictory group of settlements. Across the street is Buckman Tavern (one almost expects to see Levon with a pitcher of ale), the gathering place of the Minutemen. Three hundred and forty-four years ago, Boston was formed by immigrants whose visions seem lost. In Boston Commons, the first public park built in this country (1634), Quakers and those accused of (ideological) witchcraft were burned, or hung from a tall, arcane elm tree. At Park Street Church in 1829, William Lloyd Garrison delivered his anti-slavery speech. The first public school in Boston was commissioned in 1635, and was attended by Benjamin Franklin, Ralph Waldo Emerson, and, ironically, Cotton Mather. One reaches, touches the snow laying like cocaine powder on the cobblestones, marking the site of the Boston Massacre, the confrontation between nine British soldiers and an angry crowd, leaving dead a black man, Crispus Attucks.

And later, at Boston Gardens, 14 January 1974, there are again voices, laughter, colors, movement . . . replenishing of spiritual energies . . . expectation, anticipation . . . "As dew from the Lord, as showers upon the grass" (Micah 5:6) . . . "And the parched land shall become a pool / And the thirsty ground springs of water" (Isaiah 35:6) . . . We become the grass, the parched, thirsty ground, knocking on Bob Dylan's and The Band's doors . . . the Gardens seem old, a little tired, yet possessing, even now, a vector of energies . . . No balloons, but a low murmuring hum of conversation . . . the occasional flash of a camera . . . A sound technician is now on the relatively small wooden stage, near the brown couch . . .

9:00: Dylan on stage with The Band . . . He smiles and nods to the enthusiastic response . . . turns back . . . tuning, strumming . . . his face looks a little more tired . . .

I believe that at certain periods in a person's existence it is necessary, if not

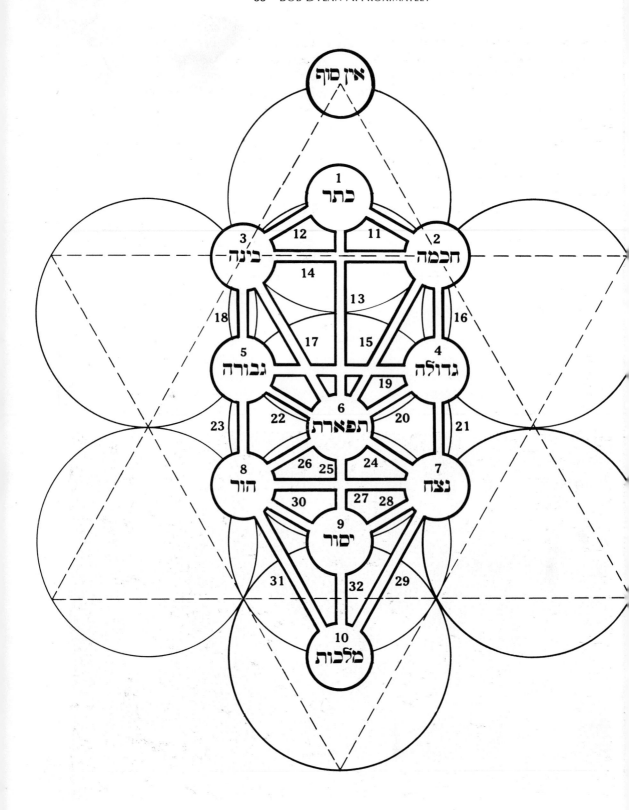

vital, to bring about a change in your life so as not to go under. I felt (after the motorcycle accident) that I needed to stop in order to find something new, in order to create—and then again I wanted to live part of my life without being continually disturbed for no valid reason. I have children and I want to watch them grow up—to get to know them, and for them to get to know me and know that I'm their father.

> —Bob Dylan to M. Enghien, <u>Super-Hebedo-Pop Music</u>, 1970.

"WHEN YOU GO YOUR WAY" . . . Dylan's voice snarling, challenging . . . "I just *can't* do what I've done before" . . . "They'll stone ya" in every possible situation . . . Dylan smiles: "Thank you. It's one of my better love songs!" . . .

The coordinator of the Boston concert is Don Law, who spoke to Ernie Santosuosso of the *Boston Globe*: "This tour is a major event for music in general. For someone to remain in America's consciousness for a decade is extraordinary. The last time I remember seeing Dylan in person was at Symphony Hall, I guess, in 1965. For this concert we're getting a tremendous variance of ages—a lot of middle-teenagers who have never seen Bob Dylan before in addition to persons in their 40s and 50s."

The Band: "I SHALL BE RELEASED" . . . The permanence of liberation; freedom cannot be extinguished in the soul . . . "light come shinin' from the west unto the east" . . . "UP ON CRIPPLE CREEK" . . . heart standing in the comic, joyful aisles of life . . . Some people dancing near the stage . . . In the dim lights, a girl silently sings the words . . .

9:50: Dylan returns in dark glasses, and everyone is shouting, then . . . "ALL ALONG THE WATCHTOWER" . . . Robbie's face animated, his fingers plucking at his

guitar, as Dylan's voice charges . . . Organ howling . . . "Princes kept the view" . . . "BALLAD OF HOLLIS BROWN" . . . Robbie's guitar maintaining a movement, an undercurrent . . . "you walk a *ragged* mile" . . . The chaos as a man's life falls out of control . . .

Hear me, O my people!
From my soul I speak with you, from the
   very depths of my soul,
from the knot of life that binds me to all
   of you and binds all of you to me,
from the sensation that I feel, deeper
   than all my life-sensations—for you,
   only you, only each of you, all of you,
   all of your souls, all your generations,
only you are the fullness of my life.
In you I live, in you, through the love
   that embraces each of you my life
   finds that fullness called Life.
                    —Rav Avraham Yitzhak Kuk
                      (trans. M. Silverman).

Dylan's left eye always seems to squint, his eyebrow raised . . . he drinks from a paper cup, his voice low and rasping, then saddened, weaving . . . "promises of paradise" . . . "Eden"—he mournfully imparts mystic portent to the word . . .

There is one who sings the song of his own life, and in himself he finds everything, his full spiritual sufficiency. There is another who sings the song of his people. He leaves the circle of his private existence, for he does not find it broad enough . . . He aspires for the heights and he attaches himself with tender love to the whole of Israel; he sings her songs, grieves in her affliction, and delights in her hopes. He ponders lofty and pure thoughts concerning her past and her future, and probes lovingly and wisely the content of her inner essence.

—Rav Avraham Yitzhak Kuk
(trans. B.Z. Bokser).

Dylan returns in dark glasses, picks up his electric Fender (the person next to me immediately notices that, since Chicago, Dylan has not used his electric Epiphone) . . . bouncing on the balls of his feet . . . "FOREVER YOUNG" . . . "May God keep and always bless you" . . . Words, prayers, the Mystery—tapping the shoulders of the collective soul of us all.

Assuredly so, whosoever is of a willing heart, may draw unto himself the <u>Shekhinah</u>, may bring her from on high, may draw her from the supernal region to reside with him; and when she comes to reside with him, how many blessings, and how much riches, does she bring with her!

—from the Zohar, II, 198b.

I *davened* today . . . I swayed, my mind danced and sang songs to the Holy King, blessed be He . . . I sang for the Lubavitcher Rebbe—may his merits be a blessing—in my dreams . . . "Patience," he said, "the Messiah will come" . . . "And if he is full of shame?" I asked . . . the question was meaningless . . . heirs to Auschwitz, we revive Nietzsche . . . a lily of the west betrayed him, Dylan has written—his light shines now in the East; he has been released . . . but his (our) responsibility remains . . . suffering, Wiesel says, is a test.

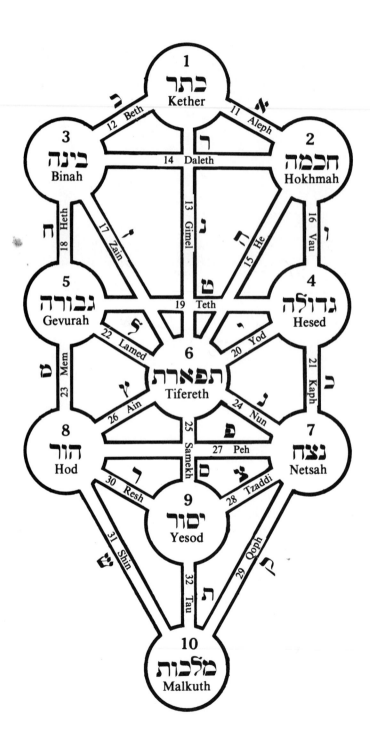

Washington, DC

Washington

Both my sons taught me to get "with it." I realized as they were growing up that I had to change also. I couldn't sit back and watch the world and listen to the new music and not be affected. My late husband (Abraham Zimmerman) and I knew that we had to try to understand the young people. We had to join in.

My son never wanted to be a super-celebrity. He is only interested in his music. When people wanted to give him honors and honorary degrees, Bob would always turn to me and say, "But, Mother, what have I really done?" There's no ego there. I love this about him. People don't understand, but he wants to live a very private, very simple life. He has a wife and five children, and he's very concerned about them. All the young people want a simple life—one or two good friends, that's all. I sometimes think that twenty years ago I should have lived the way the young people want to live today.

When Bob left school and went to try and sell his music, we were concerned about his leaving school, but we were not really unhappy. We were never alienated from him. So many people in my age group have lost their children. They wouldn't listen to their children. We listened to him. We changed.
—Mrs. Joseph Rutman (Dylan's mother).

Clear but cold air greeted the thousands who filed from the ultra-modern Capital Centre the evening of 15 January. Hours earlier, still somewhat tired, Dylan sat in his Boston Sheraton room with Tom Zito of the *Washington Post*. The black limousines which had brought the tour's principal members were parked below, and Boston shimmered in winds which penetrated even the warmest of outer garments. Mr. Zito asked how had Dylan changed.

"It's different," Dylan said to Mr. Zito, after mentioning the shared political thoughts of his early years in the Village of New York. "I look out from that stage and I can't really see who's out there. I feel that a lot of those old people are out there. I get a kick from that." The other, mostly younger members of the audience, Dylan speculated, could be attending because he may be a "curiosity" for them. Society, he theorized, has been immeasurably altered by drugs. "I mean, when LSD got 'legalized'," he told

Mr. Zito, "and everybody started smoking, everybody was getting into everybody else's head. Before that, people used to try to find out what they were all about. Drugs nipped a lot of that in the bud. It made people very passive. Now a lot of people just accept things the way they are. I've been noticing all these tall buildings in the cities we're touring. They'll just grind you down into the ground. They're monsters."

When Dylan expressed pleasure at the benefit concert for Bangla Desh, Mr. Zito asked him if he would do a benefit for a politician. "Well, there's a difference, you know. I mean, there were millions starving in Bangla Desh. George McGovern wasn't starving. He just wanted to be President." Dylan parried and avoided questions which, however justifiably those who purchased tickets had a right to ask, Dylan chose to leave unanswered. Before departing, Dylan asked Mr. Zito: "You think you could scratch out that stuff I said about George McGovern? I don't think I should go around criticiz-

ing him. I wouldn't want him to read anything like that in the paper. I think the guy's sentiments were in the right place."

Zito chose to ignore Dylan's request and the quote appeared in the Wednesday, 16 January edition of the *Washington Post*. By the time of Dylan's appearance in Washington, this embarrassment caused Dylan to refuse further requests for interviews. Zito later explained to *Rolling Stone* that "I felt it was one of the few questions where he said something more than one sentence, something that came from inside him." To me, this explanation did not made sense—anything one individual says to another is coming from one's "inside." Zito's insinuation (expressed by many in the press) that Dylan is a Jekyll/Hyde is just not true either; they just do not know how to ask questions of an individual who will not be a "news item."

Yeah, Dylan's the one who really mixed everybody up, which was definitely a good thing. It opened a lot of doors and closed a lot of doors.
—Robbie Robertson, Time, 1970.

The goal of reality, says one Hasidic teacher, of blessed memory, Rabbi Yosef I. Schneersohn, is an "elevation of creation," a unification of the "higher" soul with ourselves . . . *teshuvah*, turning, returning . . . an integration with, understanding of, the finite dimensions of infinity's manifestations . . . all of existence united with, in Rav Kuk's words, the "hovering life-spirit . . . illuminating and radiant."

Wrote Secretary of the Treasury Henry Morgenthau, Jr., on the government's knowledge of the German exterminations from August 1942 onward: "Officials dodged their grim responsibility, procrastinated when concrete rescue schemes were placed before them, and even suppressed information about atrocities in order to prevent an outraged public opinion from forcing their hand." Trains carrying *human beings* were not stopped by Allied bombers who flew overhead . . .

Capitol Centre, 15 January: A cool rush of breeze carries bluish cigarette smoke away. For the first time, thus far during the tour, the atmosphere is quiet—at least, on the surface. A candle on each side of Garth's organ glows like a cat's eyes on a summer night . . . Washington . . . Dylan sang "BLOWIN' IN THE WIND" here during the 1964 March on Washington (pale, almost fragile; *Time's* recent story on the concert in Philadelphia characterizes Dylan's newer renditions as being like a "cobra") . . .

8:26: Mr. Graham comes to the microphone, thanks the audience for its patience—a "truck problem is the reason for the delay" . . . Reading a guide for emergency exits . . . Walk, don't run. Running will affect your sex life" . . . monitor telescreens flash, then print: "At the request of the artist, tonight's concert will not be seen on telescreen."

Some arguments among people . . . many tickets marked "floor," but placed on lower levels far from the stage . . . Audience is restlessly excited . . . Far-off, I discern someone with a *yarmulka* ("It is a custom," says one rabbinic commentary, "not to walk under the heavens bareheaded") . . .

8:45: Lights off . . . single spotlight . . . Dylan/The Band suddenly appear . . . the response—beyond words . . . standing ovation . . . fast strumming of electric guitars . . . Dylan turns to his microphone, the words spitting out across the mind: "You *say* you love me" . . . "MOST LIKELY YOU GO YOUR WAY" . . . "he's *about* to call on *you*" . . . "Thank you. It's great to be here" . . .

Then there is one whose spirit extends

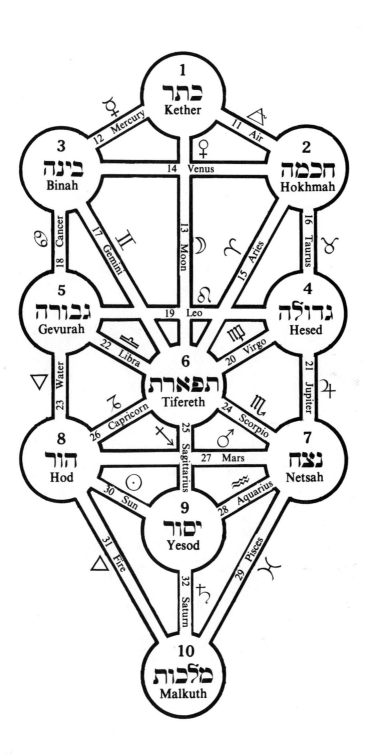

beyond the boundary of Israel, to sing the song of man . . . He is drawn to man's universal vocation, and he hopes for his highest perfection. And this is the life source from which he draws his thoughts and probings, his yearnings and visions. But there is one who rises even higher, uniting himself with the whole existence, with all creatures, with all worlds. With all of them he sings his song. It is of one such as this that tradition has said whoever sings a portion of song each day is assured of the life of the world to come. The song of the self, the song of one's people, the song of man, the song of the world—they all merge within him continually. And this song, in its completeness and its fullness, rises to become the song of holiness.

> —Rav Avraham Yitzhak Kuk
> (trans. B.Z. Bokser).

"THE NIGHT THEY DROVE OLD DIXIE DOWN" . . . In a few days, the tour will be in Atlanta—the words, so softly hymn-like (almost Anglican), bring the dualism of Tennessee mountain people to the soul (proud of the work of their hands; racist) . . . Levon's face, when he sings, is twisted in concentration . . . The fathers before us—working with our hands, our souls: racism of others has no relationship . . . The shame in knowing some were forced to kill the sons of others . . .

Dylan, from out of the darkness, steps out . . . "May God bless and keep you always" . . . "FOREVER YOUNG" . . . A hope, a wish, a gift from Jewish father to growing son . . . May we stay, yes, sustain our hearts, in shifting winds . . . "May your song always be sung" . . .

Over eighteen thousand people—from all walks of life, Jews and Christians alike—attended both concerts (15, 16 January) in Washington's Capital Centre. Away from the Centre, Dylan spent his time quietly. On Wednesday, 16 January, he visited the Phillips Collection, on 21st Street in North West

Washington. Arriving after noon, Dylan stayed until almost 3:00, walking about, looking at paintings. "Yeah, he was here," said Kevin Grogan to the *Washington Post.* "He spent a lot of time with the Renoirs and with the Rothkos."

Streams of endless craving, clinging, dreaming, flowing day and night, midnights, years, decades, centuries, millennia, streams of tears, pledging, waiting—from all over the world, from all corners of the earth—carried us of this generation to the Wall.
        —Rabbi Abraham Joshua
            Heschel, <u>Israel: An</u>
            <u>Echo of Eternity.</u>

The Wailing Wall . . . here in Washington, D.C., there, in Jerusalem? We hear the songs of tongues which, gone, come alive when we open our mouths, inhale the Mystery and exhale the present. We live in *Arabot,* the "mixture" of clouds and desert, sea and concrete jungle, of a Thin Man, of Mr. Tambourine Man, of Desolation Row—and of the Father "of whom we most solemnly praise" ("FATHER OF NIGHT").

The Holy One, blessed be He, loves this firmament more than any of the other firmaments and delights in perfecting it with supernal beauty. Therefore does it say: "Extol Him that rideth upon the skies (Arabot) . . . and exult ye before Him" (Psalm 65:8) . . . Therefore, it is written: "Serve the Lord with gladness; come before His presence with singing" (Psalm 100:2); for in His service there is no room for sadness. It may be asked, What if a man is deep in sorrow and tribulation, and has no heart to rejoice, and yet his trouble forces him to seek for compassion from the Heavenly King; is he to refrain from prayer because of his sorrow? What can he do? He cannot help being heavy-hearted? The answer is that "all gates have been closed since the destruction of the Temple, but the

gates of tears have not been closed" and tears are the expression of sadness and sorrow. Those celestial beings who are appointed over those gates of tears break down all the iron locks and bars and let the tears pass through; so the prayers of those sorrowful ones penetrate through to the Holy King, and that Place is grieved by the man's sorrow, as it is written: "In all their affliction He was afflicted" (Isaiah 63:9). Thus, the prayer of the sorrowing does not return unto him void, but the Holy One takes pity on him. Blessed is the man who in his prayers sheds tears before the Holy King.

—from the Zohar, II, 165a.

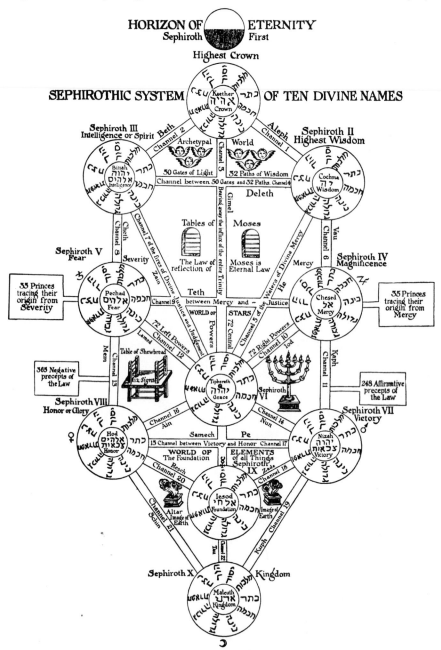

Charlotte, NC

Charlotte

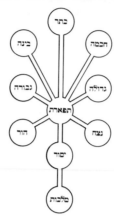

A few days prior to the tour's arrival in Charlotte, Rabbi Richard K. Rocklin shared childhood recollections of Dylan with Joyce Presley, a staff writer of the *Charlotte Observer*. "My first memory of Bobby," Rabbi Rocklin told Ms. Presley, "is when he was about five years old. Our families went to the beach together. We were as close as you could be without being related." Rabbi Rocklin called Dylan's father and mother "Uncle Abe and Aunt Bebe." When Dylan moved to New York, Rabbi Rocklin recalls, "His mother was very worried about him. She didn't know where he was living in New York, and she asked me to find him, that he probably needed money." Rabbi Rocklin was about to enter the Jewish Theological Seminary, and, in New York, he found Dylan broke and wearing "the crazy old hat" which was Dylan's early trademark. "His mother was right. He needed money." When, with Dylan's mother, Rabbi Rocklin attended Dylan's performance at Carnegie Hall, "Aunt Bebe couldn't believe it was her son on the stage. He was another person." Dylan, Rabbi Rocklin reminds Ms. Presley, "has never forgotten his heritage."

Rocklin, rabbi of Charlotte's Temple Israel also spoke with me on 17 January, before the concert:

SP: Has Dylan's poetry had an effect upon your spiritual life?

Rabbi Rocklin: I have to be frank: in one way, no. It's an enigma, because I love Bob. His mother is my aunt, and my mother is his aunt. He was my next-door neighbor. I have an I-Thou relationship with Bob. His being a star amazed me because he was my fraternity brother in college, and my wife went to summer camp with him. He used to sleep on my floor. It's a Buberian way of relating. On another level, he added substance to my life.

SP: Do you believe that Dylan's reaffirmation of his Jewish soul since 1967 will move young, perhaps disenchanted Jews to explore their spiritual beings, the roots of their Jewish souls?

Rabbi Rocklin; That's a tough one, but the answer is "yes." When Bob came by he left six tickets so I could give them to my confirmation class. It excited the kids, and instead of wanting to talk Jewish philosophy, they wanted me to tell them everything about Bobby. He'd make one helluva rabbi because he and I both grew up in homes with intense

Jewish feelings. Now he's going to Israel in March to buy an apartment. You don't necessarily have to be a praying Jew to be a Jew. Bobby never lost his Jewish roots. Israel moved him very much. He was bar-mitzvahed like all of us.

In 1968, Harold Leventhal, manager of a number of singers and actors, and Woody's friend and protector, gave Dylan some books about Israel and finally convinced him to go there. "After his father died," Leventhal told me, "Bob became quite conscious of his Jewishness. He was very excited about Israel when he got back. And it was around that time he started talking with Rabbi Meir Kehane who formed the Jewish Defense League. But before that, Kehane had been Arlo Guthrie's Hebrew teacher. Small world, huh?" ... During the Yom Kippur War, Leventhal tried to organize a big benefit for Israel at Madison Square Garden. He asked Dylan to perform, but Dylan declined. "Later," Leventhal says, "I found out that Bob had given a sizeable amount of money to Israel."

—Nat Hentoff, <u>New York Times</u>, 10 February 1974.

"The night they drove old Dixie down" ... Were the streets of Charlotte, in the winter of early 1865, a meadow which covered graves and seeds of crops alike? Did, out of the early morning fog, pale, sunken shades appear, hands asking for release? ... General Stoneman ... 10 May: the collapse in flames of Richmond, Virginia ... "But they should never have taken / The very best," Robbie Robertson's words cry out ... Robbie Robertson is across the street, at the Coliseum, but the words of his 1969 evocation (sung by Levon Helm) echo in the mind like a forgotten cantorial chant of a calliope, mournful portrait of a time ...

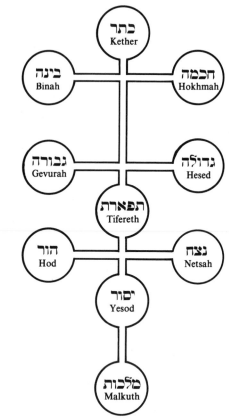

1:45: In a comfortably warm sun, Mr. Graham's enormous trucks are unloading equipment—the brown couch, drum cases, and so on. On the trucks' cab doors: a white rabbit, red-striped ears, legs blue with white stars—on roller skates. Graham's technical crew left Washington, D.C. this morning at 4:00—and the amount of work involved (lighting controls, done from the stage, and recording controls in the audience) is staggering.

7:50: Charlotte's Coliseum is small, very small, brightly lit, with wooden seats (metal arm-rests painted orange) in the balconies and mezzanine, and metal folding chairs on the main floor. Thus far, the audience's age is below twenty-five—and the Southern accents are often melodious ... From behind the stage hang two handmade banners: a brown one reading, "Everybody must get stoned"; a blue one, with yellow lettering, saying, "To Woody Guthrie, Bob and the wild blue yonder" . . . The stage is small: an electric guitar rests on a console along with a shiny brass spittoon . . . a young audience; those over twenty-five are varied, and there is one old man with a long white beard and shoulder-length hair . . . The audience cheers and laughs as two frisbees sail about and security police don't know what to do. Boos erupt when someone won't throw one frisbee when it's caught . . .

8:35: Spotlights pinpoint Dylan and The Band walking up on stage . . . Five-minute standing ovation as the musicians and the poet adjust their instruments . . . Carefully placed throughout the audience of more than 13,000 are twenty firemen and seventy uniformed Charlotte city policemen . . . Dylan turning to microphone, his face impassive, but blue eyes glancing rapidly at the au-

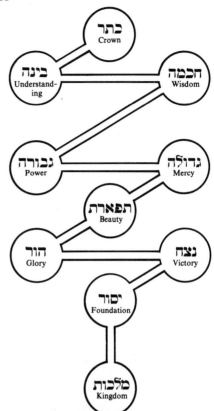

dience directly in front of him . . . the pain almost surreal . . . "I *don't* have the strength" . . . "*neither* of them are to be what they *claim*" . . .

Dylan's face a mirror of anger, honesty, challenge . . . he nods to the waving audience, turns, and walks to the piano . . . his head, for a moment, surrounded in murky candle smoke . . . "BALLAD OF A THIN MAN" . . . the geek . . . the sword-swallower . . . "how does it *feel* to *be* such a *freak?*" . . . Dylan leaning into the microphone, his face glistening . . . "an ordinance against *you* comin' around" . . . Dylan standing . . . bowing . . .

God is not less omniscient because we are taught to pray to Him, nor is He less good because He awaits our humiliation before He grants us relief; but we must assure in general terms that the expression of our wants in prayer is one of the duties incumbent on us, in common with all others; a test whether we are obedient and thereby deserving the divine favors, or whether we are obdurate and therefore deserving the continuance of the evil which afflicts us, as a just recompense for our transgressing in not recognizing the divine Power, in whose hand alone our enlargement is placed.

—Yitzhak Leeser.

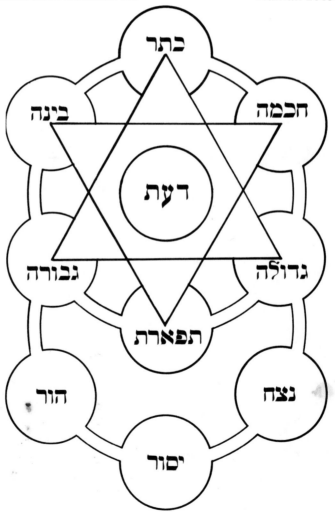

ב"ה

Hollywood, Fla.

Hollywood

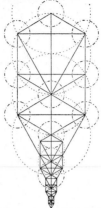

I n Miami: . . . Away from the concerts, Dylan, who stayed in a hotel in nearby Coconut Grove, ventured out to the folk and blues club, Bubba's, and, on Sunday, joined the end of a religious rally at Peacock Park. The rally was conducted by Arthur Blessit, once known as "The Mod Minister of Sunset Strip," and, according to a reporter at the Miami Herald, "Bob went up and talked to Blessit for about ten minutes. My feeling was that he was just inquiring. Art didn't want to say anything about it. He said, 'If anybody is going to talk about it, it'll have to be Bob Dylan.' "

—Paul West, Rolling Stone,
28 February 1974.

The local radio stations are warning those who attend tonight's concert not to bring marijuana, that security will be "tight," and, at the discretion of the police, one can be searched without warning. In a cover letter mailed with tickets, signed by Bill Graham and Leas Campbell, one reads in part: "Let us congratulate you upon your excellent musical taste and your good fortune to be among the small number in the entire world who will ever see BOB DYLAN/ THE BAND play music. This will be more than a concert; it will be a historical musical event." The letter's second paragraph asks for orderliness in arrival and departure; then, in the third paragraph, warns that one should not bring alcohol "and other intoxicants." The radio stations are talking, but both the (Hollywood) Sun Tattler and the Miami News have been silent about tonight's concert. So, too, have synagogue newsletters.

A warm, almost tropical, rain leaps and splatters monosyllabically upon the hot sidewalks. One stands, hands in pockets, and looks at Hollywood, Florida's modernistic Temple Beth El, perhaps the center of this southeastern area's reform community . . . Many Jews with whom I have talked are well aware of spiritual impoverishment. For some, tonight's concert will be an escape into non-identity, for others an encounter with Lubavitch Hasidism, to atone for the inner void.

In 1939, a ship, the St. Louis, left Germany with 930 Jews aboard, one of the last such ships the Nazis allowed to leave. With visas for Cuba, leaving a holocaust which burned souls daily in murky smoke, the Jews were hoping for freedom in Cuba, (the only country in the Western world which accepted them).

The ship set anchor in Havana. But suddenly, without warning, the Cubans decided the visas were illegal, that the ship had to find another port-of-entry. But no such port could be located—and, here in Florida, Jews prayed in their synagogues, stayed at the comfortable hotels, played with their children on the beach, or like all good Americans, watched baseball in neighboring parks.

Nothing was done.

"The silence is deafening," Rabbi Meir Kehane (in his provocative *Never Again! A Program for Survival*) has written of these events I am describing. "The record is obscenely empty of any vigorous sacrifice on the part of those Jewish leaders who are supposed to lead us and those Jewish groups organized to defend us . . . Franklin Roosevelt watched as 930 Jews sailed along the Atlantic coast on their way back to Hitler. He could have opened the doors and he did not. He could have saved not only nine hundred but nine thousand, nine hundred thousand. But he and all the Western democracies at whose altars Jews worshipped with such piety, did not lift a finger for the Jew. The political theory of relativity was clear: When the world is in trouble it is demanded of the Jew that he help, because he is a human. When the Jew is oppressed, humanity is freed from any obligation because it is a Jewish problem . . . And so, as the *St. Louis* came close enough to Miami for the refugees to see the lights of the city where, at that moment, Jews were laughing and amusing themselves; as the *St. Louis* mournfully headed past the American shore followed by United States Coast Guard ships under orders to prevent any refugee from jumping overboard; as the President of the United States sympathetically refused to save 930 Jews and went home, the Ameri-

can Jewish Establishment slipped silently into the night and went home too."

19 January: The Sportatorium
is suffocatingly hot; a small
metal building. There are no
seats on the cement main
floor, now solid with people who have
braved the nine-mile traffic jams (Dylan
was escorted here in his white Sports-
coach earlier today). Outside, Mr. Graham stands by the doors, watching
ticket-takers and Hare Krishna people
dance and sing. (Some, after this afternoon's concert, had gone backstage to
see Dylan, but had failed; a staff member
said that he was "tired and doesn't want
to see anyone.") . . . Someone mentions
that today is the anniversary of Janis
Joplin's death . . .

8:35: Dressed all in white, Dylan appears on stage, and is greated by thousands of camera flashes . . . For a moment he nervously rubs his hands on his
gray shirt, with white squares . . . collars
on coat turned . . . "MOST LIKELY YOU GO
YOUR WAY" . . . Dylan's voice rasping, the
words biting . . . his brown Fender shining in the lights . . . "so *hard* to care" . . .

**There are (actual people in my songs).
That's what makes them so scary. If I
haven't been through what I write
about, the songs aren't worth anything
. . . All I can do is show people who ask
me questions how I live. All I can do is
be me. I can't tell them how to change
things, because there's only one way to
change things, and that's to cut yourself
off from all the chains. That's hard for
most people to do.**
　　　　**—Bob Dylan to Nat Hentoff,
　　　　1964.**

"I was in a whirlwind" . . . Dylan nods
and smiles when someone holds up
their fingers in a V-sign . . . puts on his
dark glasses as the house lights come on
. . . slow beginning . . . then—*Wham!*

—Levon's drums explode . . . "*Once* upon
a time" . . . "LIKE A ROLLING STONE" . . .

**"LIKE A ROLLING STONE" . . . I wrote that
after I'd quit, I had literally quit singing
and playing, I found myself writing this
song, this piece of vomit, twenty pages**

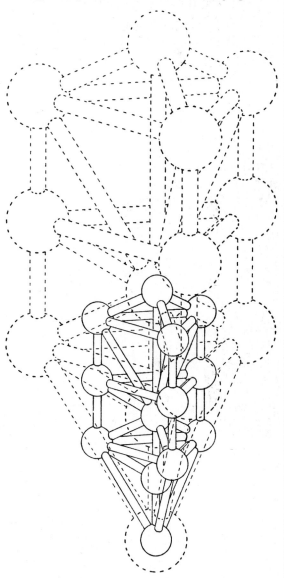

**long, and out of it I took "LIKE A ROLLING
STONE" . . . that was what I should do
(realizing a direction after the song was
completed and recorded) . . . "LIKE A
ROLLING STONE" is definitely the thing
which I do . . . a whole new category . . .**

**what I do is write and sing . . . I don't
categorize myself.**
> **—Dylan, 22 February 1966,
> Montreal, Canadian
> Broadcasting Company
> interview.**

10:55: Bows, reaching down and
touching the outstretched hand of a
young girl (she must be around ten)
. . . Almost thirty minutes later, the Sportatorium is empty, Dylan gone from the
area . . .

**Now the Sirens have a still more fatal
weapon than their song, namely their
silence. And though admittedly such a
thing has never happened, still it is conceivable that someone might possibly
have escaped from their singing; but
from their silence certainly never.**
> **—Franz Kafka, <u>Parables.</u>**

Atlanta, Ga.

Atlanta

The rich, reddish-colored soil is soaked with rain, and where the wind kisses the upper branches and needles of tall, stately Georgian pines, a mist hangs like a shadow in the mind. Just before the jet made its descent last night, a passenger (a Southern Jew who is a buyer and processor of scrap iron and metals in Macon, Georgia) told me that a *yarmulka* such as mine is not too often seen in Atlanta, that I might contemplate before wearing one in public. Then he proceeded to elaborately describe the "new, progressive Georgia" as he sat, eating his free meal (he left the ham untouched, but ate the equally *treyf* [unkosher] turkey). I thought of Pauline Kael's succinct observation that this country "rather likes its fantasies to be uninvolving." The local AM disc jockeys—few of whom have accents, all sounding like any other AM disc jockey in the country—announce that this "is the Bob Dylan weekend."

My friend Joel Rosenberg has shared these words: "It is the poet who must catch the Way. The Jew as poet who is most a Jew. But that's not all . . . We have only the shadow of understanding about what is poetry. The real name of what I mean is in disguise. A Moslem scholar says with embarrassment that Mohammed was a poet (and that the *aswak* of Mecca and the tents of Hijaz were brought with song). (I) say, as well, Jesus and Isaiah, and Moshe de Leon—that they were poets. Spinoza shows that even abstract language can become a poem, depending on one's *kavvanah* (intention) . . . There are rabbis all around us, in disguise. There are men who are pillars of the world unknown to us."

The "streets of Rome," Dylan has said in "WHEN I PAINT MY MASTERPIECE," "are filled with rubble" . . .

It is said that Rabbi Hiya prostrated himself on the earth, kissed the dust, and said weeping: "Dust, dust, how stiffnecked art thou, how shameless art thou that all the delights of the eye perish within thee! All the beacons of light thou consumest and grindest into nothingness. Fie on thy shamelessness! That Sacred Lamp that illuminated the world, the mighty spiritual force by whose merits the world exists is consumed by thee. . . . O dust, dust! I pride not thyself, for the pillars of the world will not be delivered into thy power."
—from the Zohar.

Omni, Atlanta, 21 January, 7:05: The recording consoles sit a few feet away from me . . . Dials (with needles unmoving), headphones, and two slim microphones reminding me of the steel tentacles of Martian spacecraft in *War of the Worlds* . . . Technicians on the stage are testing sound-levels . . . "One! Two! One! Two!" ringing out from behind the drums . . . The recording engineers are using a Nagra throughout the tour, the precision Swiss-made, reel-to-reel recorder, plus an Advent cassette recorder. There is a Graphic Equalizer (which breaks sound-waves into cycles, thus

symbolic heritage of my own faith by a Jewish poet—an example is 'ALL ALONG THE WATCHTOWER' drawn from Isaiah 21. 'DESOLATION ROW' has been important. The pain of being human, in his songs, strikes me in the stomach. What we all have in common is our vulnerability. It hurts, but it's not as painful if we share the experience with others. Very much like returning to Martin Buber's 'threshold experience,' returning from the Thou to the It, and the It is changed. I've got to return to my Jewish heritage as a Christian" . . .

To a roar, Dylan is coming out on

giving the ability to delete background noise on any cycle in a microphone) with its oscilloscopes (used for balance) . . . the sliders (knobs regulating every microphone's volume), below which are diagrams of each instrument. . .

Al Kooper, someone shouts to a friend, lives in Atlanta, has a studio here, but hasn't arrived on the floor yet . . . for a few minutes, I talk with Reverend Hank Night (doctoral work at Emory University; ordained Methodist minister): "From my own experience," he tells me, "it is Dylan's use of juxtaposition which is important, the breaking open of the

stage, illuminated by spotlights . . . Response is ecstatic, everyone on their feet . . . Dylan tunes his guitar (wearing dark coat, white pants and white high-heeled shoes, checkered shirt) . . . turning to microphones . . .

In the beginning, when the will of the king began to take effect, he engraved signs into the divine aura. A dark flame sprang forth from the innermost recess of the mystery of the Ein Sof (the Infinite), like a fog which forms out of the formless, enclosed in the ring of this aura, neither white nor black, neither

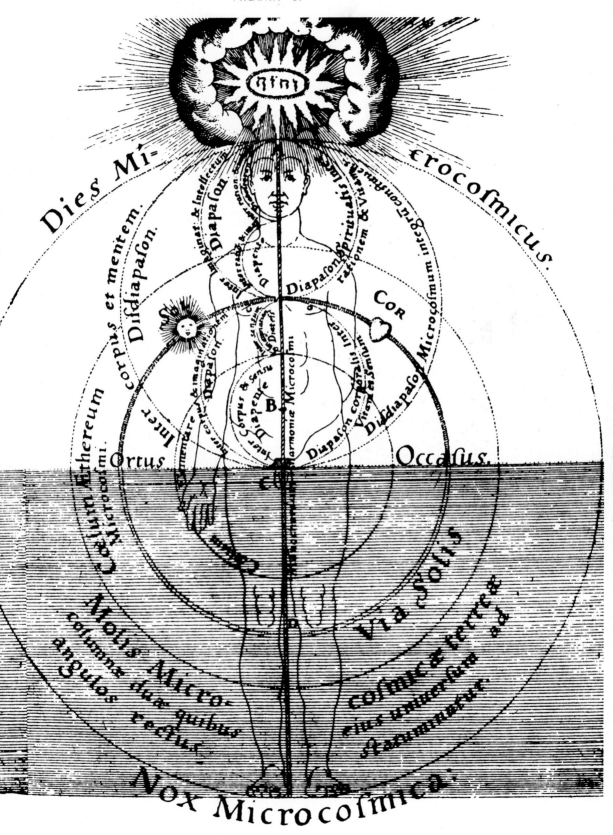

red nor green, and of no color whatever. But when this flame began to assume size and extension it produced radiant colors. For in the innermost center of the flame a well sprang forth from which flames poured out upon everything below, hidden in the mysterious secrets of <u>Ein Sof</u>. The well broke through, and yet did not entirely break through, the ethereal aura which surrounded it. It was entirely unrecognizable until, under the impact of its break-through, a hidden supernal point shone forth. Beyond this point nothing may be known or understood, and therefore it is called <u>Reshith</u>, that is "Beginning," the first word of creation.

—from the Zohar.

Robbie Robertson to *Time* (1970): "We were used to singers who opened their mouths and went 'Whop-bop-bop-lu-bop,' but Bob decided to say something while his mouth was moving,

and it was interesting to see how easy it came to him."

I spoke to Gregory Jaynes, a journalist working for the *Atlanta Constitution*. Dylan had received, in December, Governor Carter's invitation for a meeting and, last night, he accepted. His party arrived at the mansion in three black cars and was met, says Mr. Jaynes, by Governor Carter, his wife, and the Governor's family (three sons). Chip Carter, over five years ago, had gone to Woodstock to meet Dylan and, when Dylan announced the tour, asked his father to invite Dylan to their home. Through Mr. Graham, Dylan accepted, saying that he was impressed by Carter's 1972 visit to Israel. (In the 28 February issue of *Rolling Stone*, Paul West filled in more details: Chip Carter brought to Dylan a coin found at an archeological excavation in Israel.) "I asked him if he wanted a drink," Carter told the Atlanta press this morning, "but he only wanted orange juice and would only eat the vegetables." Dylan would not discuss Israel, according to Carter, but did share his feelings about his family and the tour. Greg Allman arrived shortly after Dylan had departed, to be greeted by a barefoot governor.

ב"ה

Memphis, Tenn.

Memphis

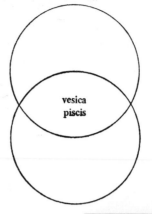

vesica
piscis

Memphis, 23 January: Gray skies, a hint of rain. This is Elvis Presley's home, and that of Jerry Lee Lewis; both (in musical areas) affected the young Bob Dylan. On the walls of Bill Graham's efficient, if sometimes cluttered San Francisco office, is a framed letter from Colonel Parker, Elvis' manager, wishing Graham and Dylan Elvis' best for the tour. Mr. Parker had also enclosed an "energy lamp," "to light your way in '74."

Before the Dylan concert, Dr. Sidney Olyan (professor at the University of Toronto's School of Social Work) spoke on Jewish intermarriage at Memphis' small, well-organized Jewish Community Center. He warned: "There is thirty-seven percent intermarriage among this generation group, and seventy percent of them cease to be Jewish families." The talk was well attended by many women (almost 400) who would later rush home or, as some did, rush to the Coliseum. "It is possible that the freedom of America is more dangerous to the survival of Judaism than Hitler's Europe was," Dr. Olyan emphasized. The "total life pattern" of being a Jew has been splintered by spiritual mech-

anization, by parents' failure to teach *and* have dialogue with their children. "But what the strengths were in the culture of the past is not necessarily right for the present," he finally cautioned.

There is, in the moving people, in the spotlights, an extension of *mesaprim*, a proclaiming of shared aspiration ... thus, it is said to those whose souls have been deadened: "Awake and sing, ye that dwell in the dust—For Thy dew is as the dew of light" (Isaiah 26:19). To Dylan's left, the edge of the stage is crossed by a Tom Sawyerish, white picket fence ... it is quiet—more peaceful than at other halls where Dylan has appeared before ... One can discern rural attitudes and rural dress (well-worn jeans, buckskin-like jackets)—costuming which, in metropolitan centers, is seen in coffee houses and clubs, in competition with the "Liverpool look" ... Someone hopes that the reserve police will not hassle Dylan, or anyone else, for marijuana—something they did at Leon Russell's last concert here ... Up until two years ago, Shelby County (Memphis being the county seat) was "dry" ...

There is only rare contact between most local people and those who come to record: Russell, at Ardent Studio; Isaac Hayes, at Stax Studios, who is seen occasionally in his gold Cadillac; and Al Green, also of Stax, who owns a lavish house, a Cadillac, and a Volkswagen ... Jerry Lee Lewis has a club here, someone says, and will occasionally walk in, playing between someone else's sets ... Presley is performing here for the first time since 1961 or 1962, someone mentions ... the security force is now massive about the stage area ...

8:34: Lights out ... Dylan appearing now—white shirt, levis, dark coat, brown square-toed boots ... "MOST LIKELY YOU GO YOUR WAY" ... the spotlights flicker,

red, white ... "You *know* sometimes you *lie*" ... His facial expressions change with each image—anger, pain humor ... "Thank *you*! It's *great* to be in Mem-*phis*!" ...

Well, what the songwriter does, is just connect the ends. The ends that he sees are the ones that are given to him and he connects them ... And in the end he'll have this composite picture of something which you can't say exists in his mind. It's not that he started off willfully painting this picture from all his experience ... That's more or less what I do.
—Dylan to John Cohen and Happy Traum, June-July 1968, <u>Sing Out.</u>

The Band: "GOIN' BACK TO MEMPHIS" ... "back in Mem-phis ... with my mama ... Chicago in the winter ... you can wear your pajamas ... goin' to the bus-*sta*-tion, goin' back to Mem-*phis*" ... "DON'T THINK TWICE" ... Shaken with changing times ... "look out your *window*" ... Dylan's knees bending as if in prayer ...

A few hours later, in the darkness and the cold wind, the party left the Coliseum, heading for Texas ...

Ft. Worth / Houston, Tex.

Ft. Worth/Houston

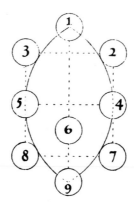

od asks for the heart of the poet, the heart of the listener. Bob Dylan asks that we give, that such a giving is reciprocal, and cannot be avoided. The heart, said the Rabbis, is the essence of all *mitzvot* (commandments). The essence of reality's planet waves is tension, duality, reintegration. We live, teaches the Zohar, in *alma deperuda*, "the world of separation." We turn to Bob Dylan— even here, in the shifting heat of Texas, where men's minds probe the stars with steel fingers of fire and oxygen—for paths that *he* has taken toward integration, for reflection of *his* soul's "echo of the wedding bells before the blowin' rain" ("CHIMES OF FREEDOM").

We ask him not for *ma'aseh merkavah* (mystic doctrine). We ask only for his voice to mingle with our voices, for *ta'ame hamitzvot*, a taste of the pathos inherent in "commandment," for in the reflection is the meaning. We cannot hide the divine within ourselves; nor can we disguise our finitude. We can search for the light in the east ("I SHALL BE RELEASED"); or we can eclipse ourselves so that no light shines ("ONE MORE NIGHT"). We can stand on the edge of a shimmering highway and see two paths:

one to the "bright lights," one "down to my grave" ("STANDING ON THE HIGHWAY"). The paths of destruction are as plentiful as those of inner re-creation.

"There's always one more notch and four more aces," Dylan has said in his powerful "BILLY 4." We can hold two cards: one the ace of diamonds, the other the ace of spades ("STANDING ON THE HIGHWAY"). We can lose ourselves on Highway 61, collapsing, spiritually dying on "crooked highways" ("A HARD RAIN'S A-GONNA FALL"). Can we continue to fail to hear Rabbi Nachman of Bratzlav's description of the laughter before dawn? Can we lose ourselves in "the depths of the deepest black forest" ("A HARD RAIN'S A-GONNA FALL")? Too many have lost themselves on the highways of death. "And bring forth our justice as the light, O holy God," says one New Year Prayer.

It is taught: "Happy is the man whose strength is in Thee; / In whose heart are the highways" (Psalm 84:6). It is said in the Talmud that, if we endeavor to sanctify ourselves, then our efforts will be successful. What occurs in this existence, occurs likewise in the existence within.

Downtown Fort Worth, Friday, 25 January: The cold air swirls and chills (even wearing heavy clothing). Tambourines and high voices, with strawberry incense, announce before one has even seen them, that followers of Krishna are nearby. The Tarrant County Convention Center—shimmering with lights and the rumble of voices and footsteps. The Children of God (one of the more fascistic of Christian groups) sell Dylan posters to those who stand in the moving lines.

"Thank you!" Dylan shouts as, with

DANNY CONNALLY, *Houston Post*

The Band, he steps into the spotlights. "*Glad* to be back in Texas!" (The jet, Starship I, arrived earlier in the day and, from the jet's passenger door, Dylan moved into the van and was taken directly to the Convention Center.) After a stomping, ecstatic version of "RAINY DAY WOMEN," Dylan leans into his microphone, smiles and shouts: "That's another *message* song!" . . .

I don't play folk-rock . . . I like to think of it more in terms of vision music—it's mathematical music.
    —Dylan, 3 December 1965, KQED-TV, San Francisco.

The backstage area was quiet. Tables were waiting, filled with gifts and food purchased for Dylan, The Band, whoever became hungry. Royce Renfro, an actor at Fort Worth's Scott Theatre (who had once been an actor-wardrobe master with Disney on Parade) was there. He had received a call earlier in the day from William Garber, the director of the theater, who in turn had received a call from Pat Knight, a member of the Stagehands Union (Mr. Knight had been contacted by the Opera Association of Fort Worth, and *they* were contacted by one of Dylan's assistants). "They need a make-up artist for Bob Dylan," Mr. Garber had told Mr. Renfro. "Report backstage at seven P.M."

Royce Renfro, with his make-up kit, arrived at the Convention Center and was promptly given a purple "TOUR 74" button. "The atmosphere was super-straight," Renfro later told a reporter of the *Fort Worth Star-Telegram*. "So quiet, like a mausoleum. Nobody raised his voice, even when something went wrong or someone got mad." At 8:00 P.M., the doors opened and, without speaking to anyone, Dylan walked into the dressing-room area. "All I put on him was a light base," Mr. Renfro related. "I blotted out the circles under his eyes and gave him a line under the eyes." Dylan was not hostile, but silent during the make-up session, and, although it did not prove necessary, Mr. Renfro stayed backstage throughout the concert.

Ibegin Kabbalah already rederanged
by times.
Time and circle stance & circumstance.
Times time: a letter-number spiral.
Watch time pass thru DvD's voice.
A song time turns around & around.
Once my voice the child voice whose
    sound was androgynous. Neutral
    tone from a bamboo flute.

Then my voice, time-tuned, intoned
young manhood, a movie & radio
voice, a web to net love with.
Now my voice is neither young nor old.
With time my voice will sound a kinder
tone. The rage is how each of us
learns to sing, to care, to make utter-
ances a way, a continuity, a bridge.
Then time will scrape my voice of its
fibers, & I will echo the whisper of
the child's voice I started with. No
beginning, no end, ancient child syllables bounced about & laughed at in
the shadows of one world transforming into another world.

A song time turns around & around. A
round. A circle.
I DvD Rumplestiltskin am loud space
between the ladder rungs.
Ring time. Bells in time are silent.
Thru time to it, back & forth. Thru it, to it.
But where is it?

I (we) want to go where?
Home? No home.
No home.
A place, <u>ha-makom?</u>
No place, no <u>ha-makom.</u>

Not here not there.
Where are the teachers we must be
before we can teach what we are?
—David Meltzer.

Hofheinz Pavilion, Saturday night, 26
January: "I'm happy to come to Houston," shouts Dylan after an opening
onslaught of "MOST LIKELY YOU GO
YOUR WAY." "Sam Houston is a personal
hero of mine!" . . . "THE TIMES THEY ARE
A-CHANGIN'," during the acoustic segment, becomes more than an "anthem"
—but a proclamative commentary . . .
"THE GATES OF EDEN"—his voice hovering like a hawk on a littered junkyard,
the wings of his symbols shadowing
illusion, illuminating truths . . . "Love,"
said one medieval mystic, "is wrath
quenched"—when one loves, then
one becomes aware of structural
weaknesses in one's surroundings . . .
Love is also a tempering of pain—and
when Dylan's face grimaces in anger
with the images of "THE BALLAD OF
HOLLIS BROWN," the Houston audience realizes that man's createdness is
coupled with inescapable responsibil-
ities . . .

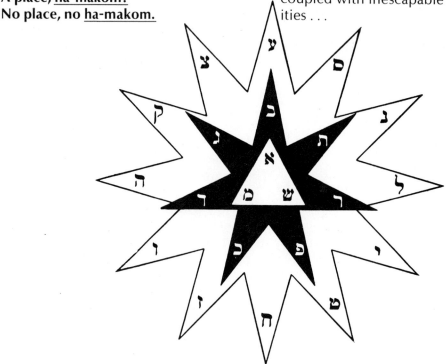

On 22 September 1965, Dylan gave a stunning performance in Austin, Texas, one of the most memorable concerts before he departed for a tour in Europe. While in Austin, he granted the interview which follows:

Journalist: What do you consider yourself? How would you classify yourself?

Dylan: Well, I like to think of myself in terms of a trapeze artist.

Journalist: Speaking of trapeze artists, I've noticed in some of your recent albums a carnival-type sound. Could you tell me a little about that?

Dylan: That isn't a carnival sound, that's religious. That's very real; you can see that anywhere.

Journalist: What about "BALLAD OF A THIN MAN"? This sounds as though it might have been dedicated to a newspaper reporter or something.

Dylan: No, it's just about a fella that came into a truck-stop once.

Journalist: Have the Beatles had any influence on your work?

Dylan: Well, they haven't influenced the songs or sound. I don't know what other kind of influence they might have. They haven't influenced the songs or the sound.

Journalist: In an article in the *New Yorker*, written by Nat Hentoff, I believe, you said you sang what you felt and you sang to make yourself feel good, more or less. And it was implied that in your first two albums you sang "finger-pointing songs," I believe.

Dylan: Well, what he was saying was, I mean, I wasn't playing then and it was still sort of a small nucleus at that time and by the definition of why do you sing, I sing for the people. He was saying, "Why do you sing?", and I couldn't think of an answer except that I felt like singing. That's about all.

Journalist: Why is it different?

Dylan: Come on, come on.

Journalist: What is your attitude toward your "finger-pointing" songs? He implied that you thought they were just superficial.

Dylan: No, it's not superficial, it's just motivated. Motivated: uncontrollable motivation. Which anyone can do, once they get uncontrollably motivated.

Journalist: You said before that you sang because you had to. Why do you sing now?

Dylan: Because I have to.

Journalist: Your voice in here is soft and gentle. Yet in some of your records, there's a harsh twang.

Dylan: I just got up.

Journalist: Could you give me some sort of evaluation as far as your own taste is concerned, comparing some of the things you like, old music, say, "GIRL FROM THE NORTH COUNTRY," which I consider a very beautiful-type ballad? Perhaps some of the things that have come out in the last couple of albums —do you get the same satisfaction out of doing this?

Dylan: Yeah, I do. I wish I could write like "GIRL FROM THE NORTH COUNTRY." You know, I can't write like that any more.

Journalist: Why is that?

Dylan: I don't know.

Journalist: Are you trying to accomplish anything?

Dylan: Am I trying to accomplish anything?

Journalist: Are you trying to change the world or anything?

Dylan: Am I trying to change the world? Is that your question?

Journalist: Well, do you have any idealism or anything?

Dylan: Am I trying to change the idealism of the world or anything? Is that it?

Journalist: Well, are you trying to push over idealism to the people?

Dylan: Well, what do you think my ideas are?

Journalist: Well, I don't exactly know. But are you singing just to be singing?

Dylan: No, I'm not just singing to be singing. There's a much deeper reason for it than that.

Journalist: In a lot of the songs you sing you seem to express a pessimistic attitude toward life. It seems that "HOLLIS BROWN" gives me that feeling. Is this your true feeling or are you just trying to shock people?

Dylan: That's not pessimistic form, that's just statement. You know, it's not pessimistic.

Journalist: Who are your favorite performers? I don't mean folk, I mean general.

Dylan: Rasputin. Hm-m-m . . . Charles de Gaulle. The Staple Singers. I sort of have a general attitude about that. I like just about everybody everybody likes.

Journalist: You said just a minute ago you were preparing to go to classical music. Could you tell me a little about that?

Dylan: Well, I was going to be in the classical music field, and I imagine it's going right along. I'll get there one of these records.

Journalist: Are you using the word classical perhaps a little differently than we are?

Dylan: A little bit, maybe. Just a hair.

Journalist: Could you explain that?

Dylan: Well, I'm using it in the general sense of the word, thumbing a hair out.

Journalist: Any attention to form?

Dylan: Form and matter. Mathematics?

Journalist: What is your belief in a God? Are you a Christian?

Dylan: Well, first of all, God is a woman. We all know that. Well, you take it from there.

A few hours before his concert in Detroit, Michigan, 24 October 1965, Dylan shared these thoughts with Allen Stone of WDTM Radio: "I've only played one place so far where I get, where I *know* there is this thing, this powerful feeling. That's when I was in Dallas, Texas (23 September) and Austin, Texas. We played concerts down there. We played "TOM THUMB'S BLUES." They knew the feeling, what it was all about. They clapped after every verse. They went wild. They didn't exactly know maybe what it was all about, but they knew the feeling of it. They were very close to it, that whole Mexican color down there. The way people *feel*."

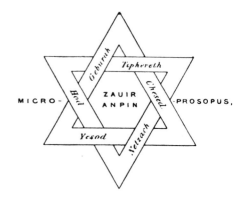

ב"ה

Nassau, NY

Nassau

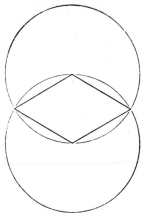

In cold, night air, thousands crowd the parking lots at the Nassau Veterans Memorial Coliseum to hear a poet share his hope. Walking earlier today: by Dylan's now-silent home in the Village, standing in front of Folk City and seeing the first photograph of Bob in New York City . . .

8:00: Last night (28 January), the rumor-machine oiled its parts, and, with Dylan's appearance only a few hours away, local television stations (without citing evidence) tried desperately to denigrate both the concert and those who would attend . . . Tickets were wrenched from people's hands, someone was allegedly stabbed, and marijuana arrests were scattered (all delivered this evening by a dull-eyed "broadcast journalist") . . . Still, among those around me, a sobering thought: in Bridgeport, Connecticut, a *shul* was burned, and only the Torah scrolls were saved . . . Tonight, it is chilly, but those in the lines are quiet, the conversations (among the young, *yarmulke*d Jews) revolving about Dylan's influence upon their souls *as Jews* . . . At a gas-station tonight, about one mile from the Coliseum, there was a fifteen-minute, screaming tirade by a customer about the fuel "shortage." The line be-hind us was enormous and frightening. Many, arriving at the Coliseum, found their fuel tanks almost empty, and they, too, joined the line . . .

9:21: The lights dim twice—and the response is a leonine roar (I can feel its vibrations in my seat) . . . Around me, everyone is visibly agitated . . . Bill Graham coming to microphones . . . "Please work with us. We'll start in another five minutes. We're all here for the same reason: to have a good time; and we want to make sure everyone is seated" . . . The candles are flickering like stars in a Montana sky . . .

Sarah Dylan, two young women, and a child come out and are seated on the couch . . . Spotlight, for a brief moment, shines directly on Sarah . . .

Dylan's words reach out, seeking the sparks we bear within ourselves, seeking a sharing. We discover that we have the potential to be *tzaddikim*, righteous ones. One Hasid, Reb Chaim Haikl of Amdur, of blessed memory, said that an ordinary man will hide his face from God's searching for man. Another man will not hide. He will stare into the glare of the Light, even at the risk of being blinded. The light is sought; yet we do not often find it. Standing in the midst of

towering concrete phalluses, or even seated in the Nassau Coliseum, it is difficult to stop and look at the Temple within, to hear the laughter—the joy—in prayer, or to feel the flames of mourning sear and tear at the soul's flesh. We light candles with which to illuminate mental paths ("SUBTERRANEAN HOMESICK BLUES," "LOVE MINUS ZERO/NO EXIT," "THE GATES OF EDEN," all carry the explicit symbol of "candle"). "In Thy light do we see light," it is said (Psalm 36:10). Even in the desolate night, the daylight of dialogues, where people may not be aware of one's pain ("JUST LIKE A WOMAN"), the *Shekhinah* is not far: "She riseth also while it is yet night" (Proverbs 31:15). It is written also: "For thou dost light my lamp; / The Lord my God doth lighten my darkness" (Psalm 18:29). In a rabbinic commentary, it is taught of this verse that God said to man: My hand is your lamp, My lamp is yours. As it is written: "The spirit of man is the lamp of the Lord" (Proverbs 20:27). Hence, the lamp of God which is our hands is for us to light. God said to man: If you light My lamp, I shall light yours.

Last night, Starship I taxied into the airport like a massive silver locust . . . Dylan spent a peaceful day with his wife who arrived from Malibu . . . Last night, Anthony Scaduto told me, Dylan and Sarah drove to their home in the Village, but went on when they saw television cameras . . .

A lounge-bar behind the stage is being used for a dressing area, a room filled with stage costumes which, one aide told Grace Lichtenstein of the *New York Times*, Dylan had wanted " in case he wanted to surprise his audience one night." "New York—it's the Big Apple," Mr. Graham told Ms. Lichtenstein. "The most frightening thing," he said to her, "about the tour so far is that nothing's gone wrong. The mood of the tour?

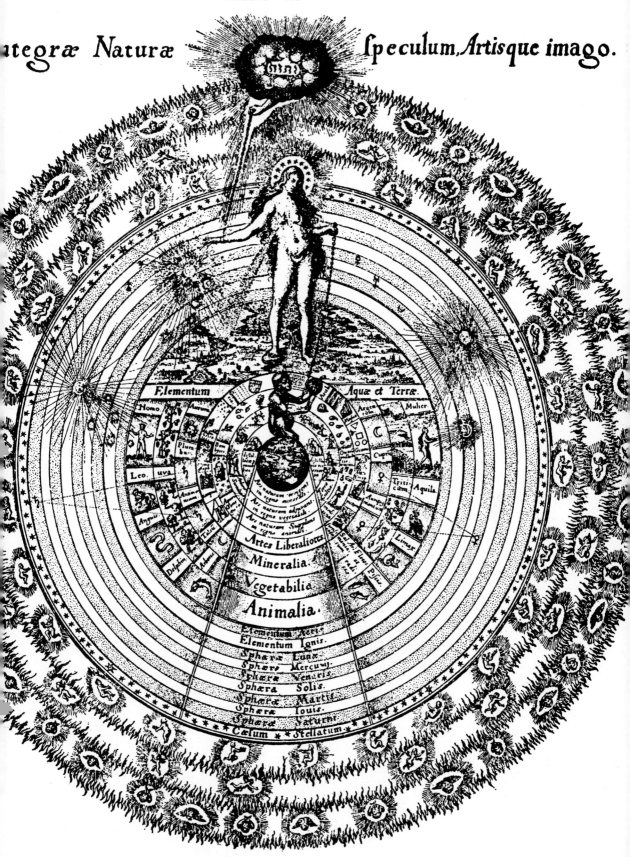

Mellow. Sounds corny, doesn't it? But I'm mellow for the first time in my life. I'm confident in the crew, the artists, and so far we've had twenty-two nice audiences." Food was ordered for the musicians. Security would be light. The fans, said Mr. Graham, "come to touch, not to pull."

ב"ה

New York City

New York City

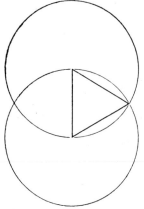

Wednesday, 30 January—opening night at Madison Square Garden; an ecstatic, powerful performance, defying scores of writers present to delineate the event. Dylan, quiet and relaxed, had surveyed the Garden earlier in the day in his fur hat, dark jacket, and aviator glasses. For a few minutes, he and The Band tested sound-levels, then he departed. Twenty-thousand people came—Hare Krishna followers danced outside, a few Hasidim (in long black coats and round hats) stood in the lines reading their prayer books. Others came as well: Yoko Ono, Carly Simon, James Taylor, Paul Simon (who sat with former Columbia Records chief, Mr. Clive Davis), Dick Cavett (who sat with Shirley MacLaine), John Kennedy, Jr., and Bette Midler.

In the smoke-filled air, Mike Porco seemed thoughtful—his Monday night jams at his club, Gerde's Folk City, provided a platform for the young Bob Dylan in 1960. (Mr. Porco had told Bob that he did not look old enough to be playing, but said that if Bob could produce identification, he could play. Dylan did.) Mr. Porco later obtained for Dylan his union card—Dylan said he had no parents so Mr. Porco became his guardian.

He gave Dylan his first professional "gig" with John Lee Hooker on 11 April 1961. Nervous and shy, Dylan sang, "HOUSE OF THE RISING SUN," "SONG TO WOODY," and a few others. His friends (and friends-to-be, such as Joan Baez) saw him and then gave him much-needed support.

Mary Travers appeared, as did Mrs. Marjorie Guthrie and Nora, her daughter. ("I was very excited and moved," Mrs. Guthrie told a journalist after the concert. "I love the common denominator of listening and music.") Also present, a happy Allen Ginsberg and a thoughtful Nat Hentoff.

In a converstaion with me, 12 May 1973, Mr. Ginsberg shared a few facts about the Ginsberg/Dylan album recorded by Apple Records, but never released. It was recorded, he said, in four sessions in late 1971. On one track, Dylan sang "Om Shalom" while Ginsberg's deep, melodious voice chanted "Om" several times. There was also "GOIN' TO SAN DIEGO," and Ginsberg sang some William Blake. Apple lost interest in the project, Ginsberg said, and he had received a message from Dylan saying that, as far as the album was concerned, the "energy's gone."

Also present: Happy and Artie Traum, who came down from Woodstock. The Traum brothers, together with John Cohen, did what is probably one of the finest Dylan articles ever published: "Conversations with Bob Dylan" (three taping sessions in June and July of 1968, published in the October/November issue of *Sing Out!*—Bob contributed a delightful cover painting). A recording session they did with Dylan had two songs ("YOU AIN'T GOIN' NOWHERE" and "I SHALL BE RELEASED," appearing on *Greatest Hits Volume 2*). They talked with Dylan briefly at the Plaza Hotel, then departed for Woodstock.

Inside the Garden, Mr. Ron Delsener, who handled the promotion for Mr. Graham, was excited and calm all at once, and Mr. Phil Ramone (who recorded The Band's 1971 New Year's Eve Academy of Music concert for *Rock of Ages*) busily prepared himself for recording all three concerts. Mr. David Geffen was excited, likewise; he was also angry. WNBC-TV had somehow managed to film parts of Dylan's acoustic set at the Nassau Coliseum, and already many have been treated by its airing on the *Today Show*.

The concert opening night was powerful, but none—not even Dylan himself—could foresee the electrical, mystic atmospherics of the afternoon concert the following day.

A man, young and petulant, began a search for a sunflower whose light was like that of the autumn sun. He searched —asking children, beggars, drunks on 42nd Street, hookers in the Bowery —but the sunflower could not be found. Then, one cold afternoon in Central Park, the man, now older, met a white-bearded Hasid who told him of the Rebbe who had thousands of such sunflowers. He raced to Brooklyn,

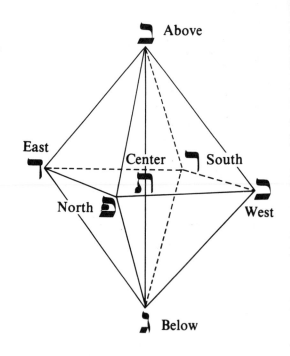

BOB GRUEN

through the imposing hallways, and rushed in upon the Rebbe. "Rebbe, Rebbe, tell me. How can you have thousands and thousands of such sunflowers, when I haven't seen one in my entire life?" "I look at the sun and see them," The Rebbe said, his eyes burning coals. "If once you have seen light, you shall always see light. Within infinity, there is further infinity."

—anonymous.

Our hands reach out to the poet on the stage, asking him to share with us the *shem hameforash*, the explicit name, of his soul's inner discoveries. As it is written: "Thou shalt surely open thy hand unto thy poor and needy brother in thy land" (Deuteronomy 15:11).

The mystics once said that the world was created when God "wrapped Himself in the garment of light" (Zohar II, 43b). "Hear, O Israel, YHVH Elohenu YHVH is one." Three Names, three

BOB GRUEN

paths to unity: how are they one? We develop perceptions of faith "in the beholding," say the mystics, "of the hidden eyes alone" that are within. We speak: an electric unit is moved in the brain, a nerve twitches, a muscle moves in coordination with other muscles, the mouth opens slightly, a breath is exhaled with control, and sound is produced. Waves of sound, vibrations, touch a fleshy appendage called an ear, reaching inside, moving parts in the skull, causing still other nerves to move, and a thought is formed. So it is with unity, with holiness, with the words of the poet on the stage enveloped in changing lights, his electric guitar an invisible wave in the air, the harmonica a thought. So it is with three names for the unity of the Mystery. Speech, say the mystics, can be an "act of unification," an act of holiness.

Eyes searching through the faces at Madison Square Garden (31 January), seeing oaths taken, a glass shattered on the floor announcing *echad*, the One, the unity of the Name. We search, the poet has said, in powerful evocations: "Drifting in and out of lifetimes / Unmentionable by name" ("LOVE IS JUST A FOUR-LETTER WORD").

3:15: Watching the faces, the needs expressed; the chaos seen outside, the "hollow place where martyrs weep," as Dylan expresses it in "DIRGE" . . .

4:10: Dylan walks out on stage with The Band—high-collared gray shirt (with checkered pattern), black coat, dark pants . . . The noise is like a sea . . . louder and louder . . . "MOST LIKELY YOU GO YOUR WAY" . . . Images crackle and eyes widen . . .

"Thank you," he says . . . half turns, then bends into the microphone: "It's an honor to be here!" . . . "LAY LADY LAY" . . . Yearning . . . touching the thoughts . . . "his hands are *clean*" . . . The evocation

of tender eroticism . . . Dylan leans into his words, almost grimacing syllables . . . Richard Manuel's white derby shines in the spotlights . . . "JUST LIKE TOM THUMB'S BLUES" . . . Hungry women, the pressure (like alien dreams) to relinquish the soul to a St. Annie, a goddess of gloom . . . "she *steals* your *voice*" . . . Dylan leans back after each verse, his Fender hammering away, then bends forward, the images rushing out in an unmistakably Jewish urgency . . . The Band, sensing Dylan's excitement, explodes forth as Dylan snaps and screams the words (this is *not* nostalgia, contrary to some; this is *not* Bob Dylan "missing" Bob Dylan) . . . Robbie's magical fingers conjuring pain . . . "I'm goin' back to New York Ci-*ty*!" (prolonged cheers and applause) . . . clapping and laughing . . . a moment passes when the song ends . . .

The name *Yisroel* literally means "he who struggles with El," with the divine: struggling as dialogue; asking (sometimes demanding) explanations from the Mystery . . . "dust is on the rise," Dylan says; blinding those who "worship loneliness" . . . The Presence is in exile, say the mystics, the Presence "lies in dust," and we search for the "living water," watching the river flow, existing in "night-darkness" . . .

Dylan immediately beginning yet another . . . "RAINY DAY WOMEN" . . . audience singing the refrains—everyone must get stoned (the song is two-faced: stoned . . . stoned, attacked, harassed) . . . "stone ya when you're in *pain*!" . . . Dylan turns, his legs spread apart, plays for those in back of him in the distant balconies and levels below, nodding and smiling . . . "IT AIN'T ME, BABE" . . . atmosphere is softer . . . "your own cho-*sen speed*" . . . Dylan bites out the challenges—"*you* say *you're* look-*in*!" . . . "a *lov*-er for your life and nothing

more!" . . . The Big Apple is a humming conclave of emotions as Dylan walks to Richard's piano (who is now on the second set of drums, just behind Levon Helm) . . . Bending his shoulders with each Halloween-like note, leaning back, looking at the distant people, who are ghostly silhouettes by the high, dimly-lit entrances . . . "BALLAD OF A THIN MAN" . . . "you go watch the *geek*!" . . . leaning back, pounding the piano . . . his eyes flickering on Danko, who stands facing him . . . 4:35 . . . his hands in his coat pockets, he departs . . . audience —on its feet, all 20,000—shouting, clapping, hands in the air—a living, breathing organism of hope and promise . . .

5:22: Dylan comes out with his metal harmonica holder . . . The Garden trembles as Dylan straps on an acoustic Martin . . . turns to microphone, nodding at those who wave . . . "THE TIMES THEY ARE A-CHANGIN' " . . . "waters around *you* have

grown" . . . Harmonica echoes out . . . his voice lingering . . . "DON'T THINK TWICE" . . . chanting the words, the harmonica supplementing . . . "good-bye's *too* good a *word"* . . . turns . . . He raises two clenched fists to those who, behind him, are clapping and cheering . . . "GATES OF EDEN" . . . "candle burning"—the candle: the soul . . . He bows and smiles . . . "JUST LIKE A WOMAN" . . . his left boot is tapping against the microphone in time to his voice and guitar . . . "she *takes"* . . . moving, extended harmonica solo, echoing and echoing . . . "her amphetamines" . . . "IT'S ALRIGHT, MA" . . . "suicide remarks are torn" . . . the words bitten out; tenacity is the only description I can think of, as Dylan, frail and alone on the stage, enveloped in lights, is shouting out at us, *demanding* of us, self-honesty . . . Then raises his left hand, waves and departs . . .

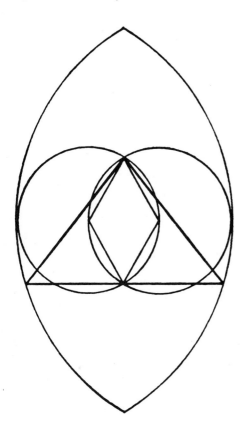

**We open our eyes
And straightway behold
The holy chariot's
Swift-rolling wheels.
Voices of song
Making lovely the air,
A joy to the heart,
A grace to the ear.
Thousand on thousand
To trembling now fall
As they sing and rejoice
From below to above
In tune with the song:
Standing who stand
Joined who are joined
In multitudes thronging,
Four hundred and fifty
Thousands of beings—
Gifted with sight are they
Yet see and see not . . .
Who sees those mighty ones
High in the Heavens
Mighty in beauty?
Who sees the Chariots
Holy and glorious?
Who sees the Hosts in
The bright courts of glory
Exalting and praising
In awe and in fear
In joy and in wonder
The Holy One's Name?**
        —from the Zohar, II, 4a.

Bob Dylan is concerned with the particulars of his Jewish reality, the *urphänomen*, the archetypal core of each night, each day. With face turned to the past, he sees man progressing: both triumphs and utter disasters. He becomes a stroller in reality, transforming meaning into archetypes, becoming a collective metaphor, giving shape and structure (intuitively) to that which is mystical/invisible. This can (and did with Franz Kafka) create existential despair: realization that language, containing the power to eradicate Creation, is often futile reification. It can lead (as it did with Arthur Rimbaud, and several Hasidic teachers) to silence. We must decide if poetic reality survives in our souls because of its subject; or, in the words of Walter Benjamin, "whether the survival of the subject matter is due to the truth content."

6:20: Lights dim . . . Thousands of matches compete with the twirling silver ball . . . Dylan returns in dark glasses . . . "MAGGIE'S FARM" . . . "sixty-eight but she says *she's* twenty-four" . . . Red roses thrown on stage . . . Dylan's eyes widen a little, and he gives the girl a big smile and laugh . . . "BLOWIN' IN THE WIND" . . . The Band singing refrains . . . Dylan turning the song into a proclamation . . . "It was great! Glad I could be here!" . . . It's incredible! Twelve minutes have passed—still everyone is on their feet, shouting, clapping, whistling, laughing . . . open tears . . . waves upon waves . . . "more! more! more!" . . . 6:45 . . . lights still on, but in the distant control booths, lights flicker . . . Dylan comes out—dark glasses, a blue "Maple Leaf Garden" shirt . . . stands there for a moment, watching and listening . . . a big smile . . . "We'll see ya next year!" . . . he waves . . . departs . . .

At nearly 3:00 in the morning, high above New York on the roof of the St. Moritz Hotel, a quiet party was being held. Dylan, listening and smiling, walked about. "I'm exhausted," he told Lois Timnick of the *St. Louis Globe-Democrat*. Dick Cavett offered him a carrot stick; he said no. Bette Midler hugged him. ("He's fabulous," she would say later—and reported in *Rolling Stone*—"I even pinched his ass.") Judy Collins, Jack Nicholson, Harold Leventhal, Lou Adler, Angelica Houston, Art Garfunkel, Clive Davis, Robbie Robertson, Mrs. Dylan, Bill Graham—all sat and relaxed. "The first part was stronger last night," Dylan said to Ms. Timnick, "but we finished up stronger tonight." Earlier in the day, on a shopping trip with his wife, some reporters tried to ask him questions. He just stared at their rudeness, then said: "Who wants to hear about somebody else's life? I'd rather go fishing." His audience? "What do they expect of me? I don't know."

Truth, said Walter Benjamin, is not "an unveiling which destroys the secret (of existence), but the revelation which does it justice." Truth, says Bob Dylan, "just twists" our illusory meanings of "war and peace" as time (the "curfew gull") rides upon clouds ("GATES OF EDEN"). In speaking of Kafka, Benjamin observed that—like Bob Dylan—"he sacrificed truth for the sake of clinging to the transmissibility" of truth, to gain the "new beauty in what is vanishing" from man's reality.

Our language—linguistic exorcisms for tongues—is that which is not spoken, but that which is thought. Language, said Benjamin, is discovered in "the metaphysically acoustical sphere," and is the essence of the reality "from which speech arises." This sphere (Is it coincidental that Benjamin, the Jewish literary critic, utilized a term found in the kabbalah?) is the language of truth: "the tensionless and even silent depository of the ultimate secrets which all thought is concerned with . . . thinking is writing without implements or whispers, silently."

Many who came from Woodstock to see Dylan's appearances in New York had not known him personally. Before his return to his house in New York, and after the 1966 motorcycle accident, Dylan remained in seclusion in the rolling hills of Woodstock.

Dylan's home on Upper Bird Cliff, one resident now recalls, was one of his favorite retreats; another home was on Ohayo Road.

"People in Woodstock are still very protective of Bob," my friend said. "These people I know have rented Bob's house on Upper Bird Cliff from the person to whom Bob had sold it. Apparently, at one time, an ABC crew had wanted to come up and photograph the place. The people who now own it said no. There's respect for his past's privacy there, and they're not into selling that past's privacy." A few anecdotes about Dylan were shared with me. The people now renting Dylan's former home came down one morning and found Dylan playing chess with a fourteen-year-old son of the family. When he realized that he was recognized, Dylan left.

"In Bird Cliff, there are lots of gardens," my friend says. "Different types, with terraces and walking paths through gardens and the woods. There's a natural spring with a natural swimming hole. One day Dylan came up with his little boy and started walking around the grounds where he had once lived. He did it a few times, and the people renting the house—about ten of them—kept seeing this man and boy walking around. Finally, someone came up to him and said, 'What are you doing here?' (And this was one of the older women who had the money to pay the rent.) He said, 'I used to live here and I want to show my son the gardens that I used to walk around in a lot.' He came back another time, and one of the older boys recognized him and started approaching Dylan, and he left. They never saw Bob again."

BOB GRUEN

Bob Dylan's poetry, his Jewish reincarnations of his life, is the music of memory; and he steals the life of the "past" from death itself. He is the manipulator of memory projected, a reflection of what Benjamin, years before "LIKE A ROLLING STONE," called "transcendental homelessness." But, unlike Kafka (tormented by spiritual stagnation), Bob Dylan does not consider man to be a suicidal, Sartrean thought of God. He does share, it would seem, with Benjamin the belief that wisdom is the "epic side of truth," which is "inherent in tradition"; that is, truth/wisdom contains a consistency of mythopoeism, and that "it is this consistency of truth that has been lost" by man.

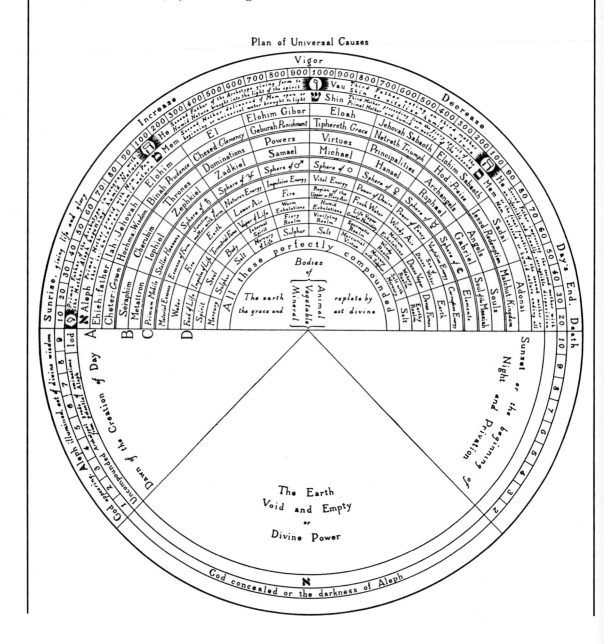

Plan of Universal Causes

ב"ה

Ann Arbor, Mich.

Ann Arbor

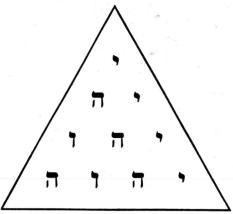

Saturday evening, 2 February, in Ann Arbor, Michigan: Almost 14,000 people cheered, clapped, and even wept during Dylan's stunning acoustic rendition of "JUST LIKE A WOMAN." Opening and closing, as he would do at many concerts, with "MOST LIKELY YOU GO YOUR WAY," Dylan and The Band coaxed and surprised the audience.

Still, there was an underlying tension. In a copyrighted story appearing the day before in the *Michigan Daily*, "Huge Scalping Racket Hits Dylan Concert," Dan Biddle and Jeff Day delivered serious charges. At the end of the concert, with some degree of anxiety, Mr. Graham came to Dylan's microphone and asked the audience for help in apprehending those responsible, citing the fact that, thus far during the tour, there had been no such well-organized racket. He was worried about the *Daily*'s charges that it was Detroit promoter Robert Bageris who instigated and guided the scheme.

"The main reason we hired Bob was to prevent this," Mr. Graham told Biddle and Day after the concert. "I'm surprised," he continued. "I can't understand it. Maybe I was wrong in my judg-ment of the guy. I trusted him." Bageris, president of Bamboo Productions in Detroit, denied any involvement, although many holding tickets said that they had been purchased from scalpers—the tickets being for Section B of Crisler Arena, the first eighteen rows. There was, said Graham, "obvious hanky-panky with the tickets. I guess hanky-panky really isn't the word. I'll say it right out: somebody was fucking around with this whole show."

Mr. Biddle and Mr. Day's original charges were explicit: "Representatives of Bamboo, the largest single promoter of rock music in the Detroit area, cooperated with the concert's bonded Detroit agent in a scheme to remove at least 300, and possibly as many as 1000, choice seats from the concert's contract-designated ticket distribution plan. The abducted tickets were then passed out to a group of at least five scalpers who offered the tickets wholesale to other sellers at prices ranging from $25 to $75 for seats on the main floor."

Mr. Graham was angered by the proportions of the operation when the *Daily*'s two investigative reporters contacted him at Madison Square Garden, Thursday night, 31 January. He said that

JOHN COLLIER

the "main concert is for the audience. We aren't doing this thing for these shmucks that wave $100 bills and rip off tickets."

When Mr. Bageris was contacted the same evening, he denied that he was the source of the tickets, but would not deny that, perhaps, some of his employees had been involved. "I really think you're barking up the wrong tree," Mr. Bageris told the *Daily*'s reporters. "To my knowledge, no one from Bamboo did anything that wasn't in the contract . . . I'm not suggesting anything, because I don't know anything. All I can say is that I didn't do anything illegal."

Those attending the concert had driven long distances to purchase tickets at the Hill Auditorium box office, 16 December 1973. However, those standing at the head of the line, with money-orders and self-addressed envelopes, would all receive either lower-priced ($7.50, as contrasted to $8.50) tickets, or would be given tickets in the high balconies. Several days before the tickets were mailed, advertisements appeared in local newspapers, offering the controversial tickets on the main floor for prices ranging from $25 to $75. It was the appearance of these newspaper ads which precipitated suspicions. Ms. Sue Young, the concert coordinator, and Mike Watts, a representative of Bamboo Productions, had delivered all of the Arena's tickets (in consecutive order, beginning with the main floor rows and ending with the balcony sections) to the box office in Detroit on 31 December. They were then picked up by Joe Variot, the bonded ticket agent, who gave them to his assistant, Frank Palaczyk. Then the main floor ticket bundles were abducted —and, at this writing, it is still unclear as to the identity of the individual(s) involved.

A few weeks after the end of the tour,

Mr. Graham told Ben Fong-Torres of *Rolling Stone* that Mr. Bageris was "a good friend, a good promoter. Because it was a college campus we didn't do mail-order, and supposedly X amount of tickets—I'd say 500—were held back for VIP treatment, and a scalper got hold of them. I haven't gotten to the bottom of that yet." (Mr. Graham's tenacity in searching out those who somehow sully his hard-earned reputation for honesty, is well-known.)

Dylan, who was aware of the ticket controversy, did not let it interfere with his performance. "Thank you," he said after an overwhelming version of "JUST LIKE TOM THUMB'S BLUE." At the very end of the concert, with the house lights illuminating memories and faces, he picked up his gray scarf, said "We're going now," threw a kiss to a fan reaching for his hand, then departed.

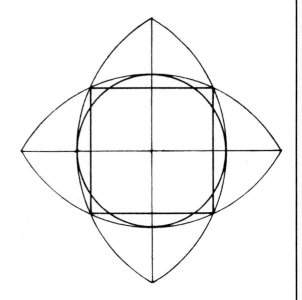

Bloomington, Ind.

Bloomington

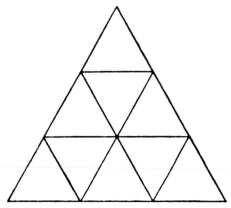

Sefirot, emanations of Light, formed and articulated as song and poem, dance for one's eyes. The Band, shimmering images in spotlights, create mathematic laughter and whispered tears; and Dylan, moving before one like a *tzaddik* on fire, gives the summation, showing the listener how his soul has transcended the malapropisms of an age.

In the sefirotic forms of poetry, God is hidden; yet made manifest for those who will search. "You are He," says the *Tikkune Zohar*, "Who binds them, who unites them." In the *sefirot*, we discover who we are, and who we are not. We discover, in Dylan's description, that "I'm not loving you for what you are / But for what you are not" ("I'LL KEEP IT WITH MINE"). We discover in Dylan's calls to the divine, the "Origin of Origins, the Cause of Causes."

We can be wise, but our wisdom cannot schematize the divine. We can understand, but our understanding cannot grasp the infinite. We search for the Father of Night; for what one kabbalistic master, Rabbi Elazer Azkari of Safed, of blessed memory, called "Father compassionate, Heart's companion."

The Psalmist asked: "Who can express the mighty acts of the Lord / Or make all His praise to be heard?" (Psalm 106:2). Dylan has provided one possible answer: "So don't fear" the "foreign sound" which will come to one's consciousness ("IT'S ALRIGHT, MA"). We turn to the Voice with silence and hope, the former the language of the soul, the latter that of the spoken word. "The preparations of the heart are man's," it is said, "But the answer of the tongue is from the Lord" (Proverbs 16:1). Dylan warns, however, that the wicked messenger will precipitate disaster: "For his tongue it could not speak, but only flatter" ("THE WICKED MESSENGER"). "For there is not a word in my tongue," it is said, "But, lo, O Lord, Thou knowest it altogether" (Psalm 139:4).

"The pursuit of meaning is meaningless," wrote Rabbi Abraham Joshua Heschel, of blessed memory, "unless there is a meaning in pursuit of man." Both God and Bob Dylan search for each other. The discovery of the One for Dylan is the force behind his poetry.

The Assembly Hall, 3 February: A small but high building with steep inclines on two sides; cushioned, red and blue seats on two sides; wooden

small-town, Bible-Belt audience (albeit also a university town—boasting one of forty-seven known copies of the Gutenberg Bible) . . . There are excited cries of greeting between friends . . . cowboy hats . . . a 4-H coat . . . Those with shoulder-length hair (a minority; many here have wire-rimmed glasses, boots, and crew-cuts) are dressed in slacks and new shirts and coats . . .

8:25: Darkening . . . Tremendous welcome as Dylan and The Band file up on stage . . . "MOST LIKELY YOU GO YOUR WAY" . . . the acoustics are poor—the sound, at times, seems muffled . . . "you know you're not *that* strong!" . . . "Thank you! Sure is nice to be here!" . . . Dylan, spotlighted in red, moves like a ballet dancer . . . "started out on burgundy"—everyone applauds . . . cheers, claps in time, and then immediately begins . . . "RAINY DAY WOMEN" . . . "stone ya when you're livin' in the *sticks*" . . . "stone ya when you're standin' at the *bar*" . . . Dylan

benches on one; metal folding chairs on the main floor; and no seats behind the small wooden stage . . . One has the sensation of being at an assembly hall, but instead of a mahogany podium for an inevitably sanctimonious speaker, there are silvery microphones, a tapestry, and vehicles of evocation for a

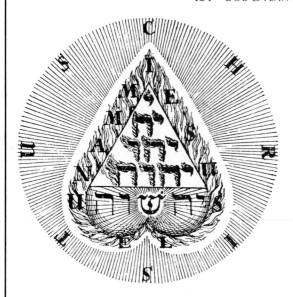

breaks a string and a technician runs for another guitar . . . "JUST LIKE A WOMAN" . . . Another string breaks as he sings part of the first verse . . . He puts down the guitar . . . stands for a moment . . . is handed yet another guitar . . . tunes it . . . turns to microphone . . . "I did it once. The whole last song with a broken string. I want to get it right this time. I'm glad to be here. I'm glad to be any-where."

St. Louis, Mo.

St. Louis

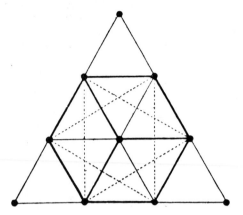

Others may praise what they like: But I, from the banks of the running Missouri, praise nothing in art, or aught else, till it has well inhaled the atmosphere of this river, also the western prairie scent, and exudes it all again.
— Walt Whitman.

A wintry wind touches the highest leaves, then dances about street-corners which, like children in an imaginary Maxfield Parrish poster, shiver in the nights. The tour ends in ten days. The two enormous trucks will depart with their lighting and sound equipment for other destinations. There are no Hasidim in St. Louis. On the outskirts of town, as in Bloomington, Indiana, are bars where the cowboys told me they would not shoot pool for beers (which I don't drink), but "only for joints, man," and marijuana is something I rarely touch. The cowboys are friendly here, although a little distant; perhaps a beard and a *yarmulka* are pale comparisons to their carefully folded hats and ruddy-colored boots. The cowboys, lounging at the bar, attack Richard Nixon—not for being "soft" on communism (many of them are ex-Navy people and have seen that "communism" is not monolithic), but for being such a "damned crook." One sips a whiskey sour, glances at me, keeps drinking; all that was missing was a Colt at his side and a horse outside. Time stands still, it seems, within a Missouri bar. A few college fraternity brothers are here, trying to "slum a little," but one seriously questions if their historical senses are being nurtured. I watch a cowboy wipe his lips with his sleeve, pick up a copy of the *New Yorker*, and walk slowly to his 1956 Ford and disappear into the cold night, his radio loudly blaring the local country-music station . . .

The Jewish mystics talked of song. They talked of the Messiah's home being "from that place called 'The Bird's Nest' (this 'bird' is the *Shekhinah*)." The time of his coming would be the time of a light shining from the west unto the east: "A star shall come forth from the East variegated in hue and shining brilliantly." The star would wage war against the children of darkness with the weapon of illumination, and concerning this time it is said: "For behold, darkness shall cover the earth / And gross darkness the peoples"

Iconismus inserendus Tom. II Fol. 287
Speculum Cabalæ mysticæ
In quo omnia, quæ Hebræi de nomine
dei tetragrammato arcanè retulerunt,
ys ad nomen messiæ Iesu respexisse de-
monstratur. Omnes quoq; mundi nationes
nomen dei non sine mysterio
4. litteris enunciare, docetur.
Explicatur in Cabala fol. 287

(Isaiah 60:2) . . . "Darkness at the break of noon" ("IT'S ALRIGHT, MA").

When the Messiah weeps for the world, the Holy One, blessed be He, beckons to the Bird, which then enters its nest and comes to the Messiah, and flits about, uttering strange cries. Then from the holy Throne the Bird's Nest and the Messiah are summoned three times, and both ascend into the heavenly places. And the Holy One, blessed be He, swears to them to destroy the wicked kingdom by the hand of the Messiah, to avenge Israel, and to give her all the good things which he has promised her. Then the Bird returns to her place. The Messiah, however, is hidden again in the same place as before.
—from the Zohar, II, 7b–8a.

It is said that when Rabbi Jose, the Jewish mystic, had reached old age, he remembered words spoken by his father. That, when one becomes sixty years of age, one will find a "treasure of sublime wisdom." Now, Rabbi Jose was filled with doubt. His father also said, eyes gazing at the city of Jerusalem, "When the celestial flame reaches the spaces between your fingers, it will escape from you." "How do you know this?" the young Jose asked. The father squinted at the innocent eyes of his son. "I know it by the two birds that passed over your head."

Jose could not understand. He walked along, found a deep cave and entered, finding a book in a rocky cleft. The book was large, yet small; old, yet new. One page was filled with the "seventy-two tracings of letters which had been given to Adam the first man, and by means of which he knew all the wisdom of the supernal holy beings, and of all those beings that abide behind the mill which turns behind the veil among the supernal ethereal essences, as well as all that

is destined to happen in the world until the day when a cloud will arise on the side of the West and darken the world."

Rabbi Jose and Rabbi Judah sat down, their voices raised in elation. They began studying the first three of the seventy-two letters. Suddenly, a "fiery flame driven by a tempestuous wind struck their hands, and the book vanished from them." Rabbi Jose began weeping, thinking that, God forbid, they had somehow sinned by studying those first three letters.

The two rabbis went to a mentor, Rabbi Simeon, whose mystic knowledge was known all over the Jewish world. "Were you, perhaps, scrutinizing those letters," Rabbi Simeon asked, "which dealt with the coming of the Messiah?" The two shook their heads, saying, "We cannot tell, as we have forgotten everything." Rabbi Simeon gazed at them, his eyes keen. "The Holy One, blessed be He, does not desire that so much

should be revealed to the world, but when the days of the Messiah are near at hand, even children will discover the secrets of wisdom and thereby be able to calculate the millennium; at that time it will be revealed to all, as it is written, 'For then will I turn to the peoples / A pure language.' "

All of reality is a reflection: the placid creek of clear water reflects not only that countenance of the child, but also that of the "angels who play with sin." We contain, within, totalities of Light, *sefirot* (emanations of light), as well as the fragmented realities of our existence. We are *adam ila'ah*, "man above." A few doors from where I am writing these words, Bob Dylan sleeps, The Band sleeps. May God give their music tonight a taste of eternity. The great medieval Rabbi Loew of Prague (who, as legend tells it, created a Jewish Frankenstein, the Golem) once said: "Faith, believing in God, is attachment to the highest

realm, the realm of the Mystery . . . for what is highest is hidden." Hidden, but which can, for a moment through song, be touched.

9:40: St. Louis Arena, 4 February . . . It has been said that man must discover the fires of his soul and must, as well, shield himself in order not to be "burned" by the intensity of the Source . . . If a man, if a poet, fills the void in his soul with Light, then all is re-created within him; if man be consumed by chaos, then the abyss yawns before him . . . The poet seeks *bittul hayesh*, "annihilation of (chaotic) somethingness"; he seeks (and shows) *yesh*, "that which is," even if "this" be chaos . . . Has not an inner discovery of "planet waves" given the poet visions of *nefesh ha'elohuth*, the divine soul? The *nogah*, the brightness, is man's natural soul, which contains, teach the Hasidim, an actual portion, a "spark" of the divine soul . . . Seeking to obliterate shadows, Dylan, the poet, gives us two of God's gifts: song and laughter . . .

The Arena, a massive steel-concrete Moloch: the house of hockey in St. Louis, the dying industrial "gateway to the west" . . . The stage is small, but no one talks of the stage's organization: there is talk of Leon Russell; of St. Louis' garbage strike ("Just wait," a young girl says, "Wallace is gonna solve it"—she is serious) . . .

The concert: As in Philadelphia and at the afternoon concert in Madison Square Garden, Dylan reaches out and within . . . "MOST LIKELY YOU GO YOUR WAY," "LAY LADY LAY," "JUST LIKE TOM THUMB'S BLUES," "RAINY DAY WOMEN" . . . Leon Russell walks on stage in his cowboy boots and, holding a cup of wine, waves his hat at Robbie Robertson . . . Dylan smiling, laughing . . . "Leon Russell!" he shouts to the already propitious

audience . . . "IT AIN'T ME, BABE," "BALLAD OF A THIN MAN"—Dylan *pounding* the piano with lyrical invectiveness . . .

The acoustic segment: Dylan—his face set in his grimace, his voice running an implacable array of emotions . . . "THE TIMES THEY ARE A-CHANGIN'," (his harmonica chanting angrily like a rabbi at the Wall) . . . "DON'T THINK TWICE" . . . "WEDDING SONG"—his voice powerful, straining . . . "now that the past is *gone*" —the last word held, and everyone shouts . . .

Russell comes out, stands watching, hands behind his back . . . Dylan smiles as Russell puts his cowboy hat on Dylan's head . . . Dylan motioning for Russell to sing with him, then tosses the hat back on Russell's head in one motion . . . "Thank you! It's been a long long time! Thank you" . . . Just as quickly, Dylan and The Band return . . . "MOST LIKELY YOU GO YOUR WAY" . . . smiling . . . "Thank you! Good night!"

Watching the river flow . . . Dylan, standing in a blue spotlight, his acoustic, steel-stringed Martin reflecting, for a thousandth of a second, the face of a young girl whose eyes are filled with tears at tonight's concert . . . Robbie Robertson, leaning over his Fender, smiling, his eyes closed, fingers moving like the font on an IBM selectric typewriter . . . and Levon Helm watching, grinning, as Dylan's voice soars with "FOREVER YOUNG" . . . watching the river flow . . . "The voice of the Lord is upon the waters" (Psalm 29:3) . . .

Denver, Col.

Denver

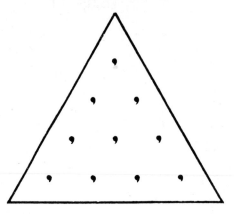

An American Jew, who hailed from Denver, Colorado, once visited the Chief Rabbi in Jerusalem (Rav Avraham Yitzhak Kuk) and complained to him of the irreligious activities of the secular pioneers in the new communes. The Chief Rabbi affected to ignore the complaints and, in an apparent effort to change the topic of conversation, inquired what kind of city Denver was. The American began to tell with exuberant civic pride of the marvelous climate of that great city and its world-famed hospitals. With seeming naiveté, Rav Kuk remarked, "I heard that Denver was filled with tubercular people. Does it not mean that it is an unhealthy city?" "On the contrary," replied the Denver Jew smilingly, "because of Denver's wonderful climate tuberculosis hospitals have been established in it, and the sick people from the whole nation come to live there." "Even so," replied Rav Kuk, "sick Jewish souls from all parts of the world come to sink their roots in the Holy Land, there to be renewed and invigorated."
> —from Rabbi Jacob Agus, Banner of Jerusalem: The Life, Times, and Thought of Avraham Isaac Kuk.

Denver Coliseum . . . 6 February: Snowy paths in both streets and minds, freezing everything . . . People talking, hands rubbed and blown upon—walking to heart and soul's light . . . Among the many Jews here tonight is a yearning for flickers of *reshafim*, sparks in the soul . . . of *memalleh kol almin*, the Immanent . . . of *sovev kol almin*, the Transcendent . . . *kimnagen hamenagen*: "and when the minstrel played"—of Johanna, of Queen Mary, of wedding song, and spiritual dirge . . .

10:31: Dylan, Levon Helm, Robbie Robertson, then Garth Hudson and Rick Danko, walking on stage . . . "Thank you! Full moon tonight!" . . .

In every second, in the smallest instant of time, we create, consciously and unconsciously, an endless multitude of creations; if we can only learn to perceive them, bring them within the borders of clear cognition, accustom ourselves to include them within the framework of expression suitable for them, then their splendor and majesty will be revealed and their power in all phases of life will become visible.
> —Rav Avraham Yitzhak Kuk, "The Experience of Mysticism."

A large party backstage after the concert . . . Eighty-proof, homemade Tennessee grape wine passed around . . . Richard Manuel leaning back in his chair, laughing, then unable to stop . . . For a while, Dylan plays a fast game of ping-pong, his aviator glasses reflecting all . . . Stops and kisses a young three-year-old girl who is carried backstage by a guard for her mother . . . The next day, at Denver's Playboy Club, Dylan and The Band begin thorough rehearsals of new material they hope, somehow, they can use for the closing concerts of the tour . . .

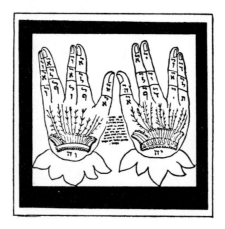

Seattle, Wash.

Seattle

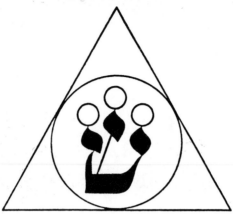

S eattle Coliseum . . . 9 February: *Orot ha-kodesh*, lights of holiness, touch our hands and faces, tightly fitted around the stage . . . Listening to the cachinnations of the waves beating against the Pacific Coast, echoing within the minds at this Coliseum . . . Thoughts become languages only the living can understand . . . voices slow and hovering over moonlit stage . . . The mind: *mysterium salamandrae* . . . aleph, aleph . . . *bereshit*: Creation . . . *ahavat Yisroel*, love of Israel, warms my cold, shaking hands . . . Come, my brethren, draw the circle, the circle; come my brethren, draw, draw;

come, my brethren, come . . . the circle, circle, circle . . . Said one Talmudic sage: "Know before Whom ye are standing" . . . knocking . . . "And He commanded the skies above, and opened the doors of heaven" (Psalm 78:23) . . . Intracosmic realizations . . . Dylan and The Band are quietly eating backstage in the dressing room . . . Wally Heider of Los Angeles has his remote sound truck in back of the Coliseum . . . There is a video monitor by Dylan's microphone . . . For the first time since Miami, I receive a *shalom*—from two Jews: one Canadian, the other born in Algiers and raised in Jerusalem . . .

8:12: Blue lights on stage . . . house lights off . . . Dylan appears . . . smiling . . . a blue flag in his hand . . . a green medallion on his coat lapel . . . "MOST LIKELY YOU GO YOUR WAY" . . . "Thank you! Glad to be in Seattle! Home of Jimi Hendrix!" . . .

Oakland, Calif.

Oakland

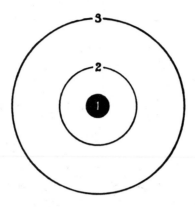

Rabbi Schneur Zalman, of blessed memory, taught that if one fails to discern the fractures of reality, he is "incompletely righteous," he is "a righteous man who suffers." In his words, we envelope ourselves in "folded garments." In our hearts are fragments of the absolute life: we strive for covenants, for reintegration of our souls in a society grown meretricious, for what Martin Buber termed "true community," something not found, he said, in the dream-like essence of "prescribed forms." We become Daniels, realizing humanity, grasping at certitude and impotence, the laughter of painted clowns and the tears of silicone ephemerals. Blanketed in fog, San Francisco beckons to the poet: in saying *thou*, we have learned to say *we* . . .

. . . hair, like thin brownish wires standing out from his head, (he) stood at the microphone, raising himself on tiptoe to mark the emphasis of a word or an accent singing the familiar songs . . . It made a great sight. Here was one of America's greatest singers (who is also America's greatest poet) standing there like an I. Magnin mannikin clutching an electric guitar, backed by racks of amplifiers, loud-speakers, a piano, another guitarist, an electric bassist and a drummer, and overhead, making a surrealistic stage set, four paintings by Bob Neuarth. In each painting, from the space man to the rock 'n' roll players, the figures were an abstraction of Dylan's own image, or so it seemed to me after two glasses of milk and a Hershey bar . . . It is a loud band, but an exciting and delightful band full of kicks and flashes of great moments. It is obvious Dylan blows his mind playing with them.

—Ralph J. Gleason, <u>San Francisco Chronicle</u>, 30 November 1965.

Oakland Coliseum, 11 February: Thousands of automobiles are rushing toward the gargantuan sports complex, set in the midst of a concrete parking-lot. Even before the concerts, however, a few voices formulate questions about the tour: some of them are, to be sure, lethargic; others, set in sagacious terms, deserve discussion.

In Dallas, Texas, after a performance at 57 Doors during the first week of December, Mimi Farina announced that she was going to picket the two Oak-

land concerts. She—like others who demanded too much of a shy poet throughout the years, as Anthony Scaduto has aptly documented—was bitter toward Dylan's alleged "desertion" of political activity, and accused him of worshipping fame and fortune. "He'd been kind of a pushy, Jewish fat kid," she expostulated. "But he was also cute and a genius at the same time. And when that period was over, he seemed to lose all care and respect for himself and for life in general, and he eventually disappeared and stopped performing altogether."

She also accused Dylan of having vanquished "his sympathy towards human beings," by charging high prices for tickets. (The fact that, as Ralph J. Gleason later estimated, one was actually paying only forty-five cents per song did not seem to enter her mind.) In the 8 February issue of the *San Francisco Chronicle*, she took her feelings a step forward and published a short open letter to Dylan. "There is an important question," she wrote, " . . . concerning the profits of your tour. Rumor has it that a portion of the five million dollars to be grossed by the tour is going to Israel. That doesn't seem a likely assumption, partly because of the $2.2 billion the US has already given Israel for armaments, but also because of your compassionate understanding for those who suffer. (She seemingly forgot her comments in Dallas, Texas.) In a time of war, when God is on neither side, clearly both sides suffer spiritually and physically. To financially encourage one side or another is to encourage war itself regardless of who starts it."

Jeremy Larner, author of the screenplay for *The Candidate*, had visited Israel since the Yom Kippur War. He answered Mimi Farina in the 15 February issue of the *Chronicle*. He began by

pointing out that it is illegal for an American citizen to donate money for purchasing of arms; that, should Dylan donate money from the tour, it would most likely be utilized for medical, educational, and agricultural needs. "Israelis do not get arms from Bob Dylan," he continued, "and other friends around the world—they get a portion of what they need to keep their society going in the face of continuous violence from their neighbors. Perhaps you should know, Ms. Farina, that along the Lebanese border, shells from guerilla bases fall daily among Israeli farms and towns, that in certain areas a whole generation of Israeli children have grown up sleeping and going to school in bomb shelters. Does it seem strange to you that Bob Dylan might contribute to the well-being of his fellow Jews under these circumstances? Would you deny him a human response you would grant to a member of any other ethnic group?

You wouldn't object, I assume, to a black entertainer giving to a breakfast fund for Oakland children; why can't Bob Dylan buy some breakfasts for needy Israelis?"

In the last part of his letter, after pointing out the tyrannical nature of Arab sheikdoms (which can hardly be considered "oppressed" by the Jews), Mr. Larner concluded: "Do the Israelis have any reason to believe that defenselessness would not very swiftly cause a great deal more suffering—including that 'physical' form of suffering known as death? You must admit, Ms. Farina, that the history of this century is not encouraging about what happens when nations capitulate to well-armed anti-semites. So far, it has always turned out that they mean exactly what they say."

What the world cannot forgive Israel is her determination, both daring and irritating, to remain human in a situation which is not . . . By affirming that man—any man—is more important than objects—any objects—Israel irritated public opinion. Please, do not protest: that's how it is, that's how it has always been. People used to hate the Jew because he refused to fit their concept of a victim. Today they are disturbed because he refuses to fit their concept of a victor. He has dared to undertake, and successfully, a perilous operation—the temporary seizure of an enemy airport (in 1967)—without causing a single injury. Admit that there is something in that to offend his judges . . . When Israel is on trial, everybody stands up to be counted. Then all have something to say. Why are they so eager? Because, to them too, Israel remains a people apart, a people whose very existence constitutes a challenge to richer and mightier nations. Whose way of conducting wars and winning them is a reproof to those whose own battles brought no glory to the human spirit.
—Elie Wiesel.

10:15: Yellow daisies in the spittoon by the organ; on each side, smaller bouquets of white and yellow flowers . . . Lights dim twice . . . Oakland Coliseum: ultra-modern, with over-worn wooden floors . . . constant feedback from speakers . . . Rapidly filling with a noisy, whistling crowd . . . Candles . . . frisbees flying to cheers, moans, applause—must be six or seven of them . . . members of the Grateful Dead, Santana, and the Airplane are here . . . Annie Leibovitz, the chief photographer for *Rolling Stone*, walks hurriedly by . . . Joan Baez and sister Mimi sit pensively . . . Ralph J. Gleason is all smiles . . . Robert Hilburn of the *Los Angeles Times* walks about, watching and listening . . . Soap bubbles floating precariously . . . a frisbee almost hits a technician, who

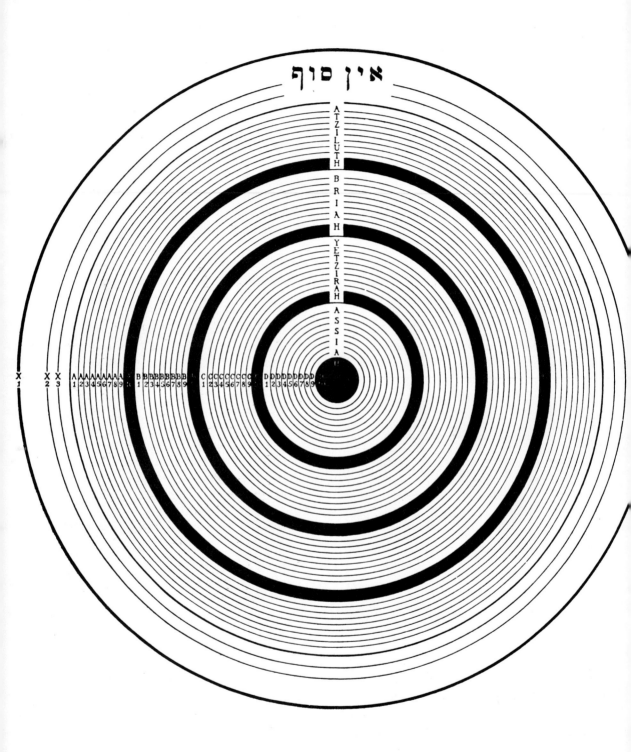

throws it on the floor backstage . . .
lights out . . .

**This is the New Song, the New Youth,
and it speaks in images and poetry and
its voice is louder than anything we have
heard before. I played portions of the
new Dylan album (HIGHWAY 61 REVISITED)
for a young man studying for the
priesthood. "He's a preacher," he said,
"he ought to be speaking in the cathedrals." He is. It's only that the cathedrals,
too, are different.**
> —Ralph J. Gleason, <u>San Fran-
> cisco Chronicle</u>, 19 Sep-
> tember 1965.

10:30: Blue spotlight on stage . . . Dylan appears first, in white shirt, black
pants, vest, and coat . . . Everyone
standing . . . then . . . "MOST LIKELY YOU
GO YOUR WAY" . . . Dylan biting out the
words . . . "let you *pass*" . . . Naked contempt in the images . . . The Band exploding . . . Legs spread, Dylan sways
like an Israeli palm . . . voice becoming
more savage . . . Audience stunned by
the velocities . . . "and I go *mine*!" . . .
"Thank you! Great to be back at San
Francisco Bay!" . . . his guitar begins,
progressively higher . . .

**Compassion, humanity, and a passion-
ate determination not to surrender to
compromise mark his attitude and his
poems. Like Lenny Bruce and the jazz-
men, what Dylan does is done from the
heart, "you don't lie." The confusion that
some have experienced because of his
recent involvement in personal expression is due to their insistence that his
poems are issue songs whereas, even
when they are concerned with issues,
they are actually morality poems on
every level and in every aspect from the
personal to the universal.**
> —Ralph J. Gleason, <u>San Fran-
> cisco Chronicle</u>, 6 Decem-
> ber, 1965.

The view of a man going mad—going
"normal" in a mad situation . . . Dylan's
intensity staggering—as he stands, almost immobile, shouting out his poem's
anguish . . . words snarled out . . . a quick
departure . . . Smiling as he sees the
thousands of matches . . . the reflected
faces in his dark glasses . . . Someone
throws a hat to him . . . he smiles, turns,
tosses it to Louie Kemp . . . "BLOWIN' IN
THE WIND" . . . an anthem, perhaps, a

declaration of independence, and our
dependence upon another, upon our
ability to hear the winds . . .

**I'm just a retarded ex rock 'n' roll forbid-
den fruit picker writin words to keep
time always at my come as you are party
. . . will see you in San Francisco . . . am
plannin to make grand entrance during
hard rainstorm in my blowin in the wind**

tee shirt (about midnight) . . .
     **—Ralph J. Gleason, <u>San Fran-</u>
     <u>cisco Chronicle</u>, 6 Decem-**
     ber, 1965.

Dylan, The Band, and Bill Graham
were in Mill Valley during the last few
days—a quiet area, trees, paths, with
many brilliant artists there. They were
seen, relaxed and fulfilled, at the Tri-
dent, a dockside café in Sausalito, and
later at Mr. Graham's offices. In a few
hours, they were heading toward the
Inglewood Forum where, in late December, they had performed their first
sound-checks.

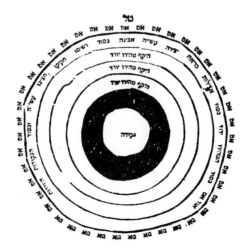

Los Angeles, Calif.

Los Angeles

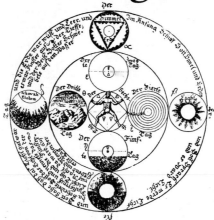

The ghost of Raymond Chandler walks phantasmal Beverly Hills, and Link Davis' Cajun fiddle echoes around the La Brea Tar Pits . . . A city of angels playing with sin, the purple haze of the ozone sun all in dreams and silver seeds . . . The horseman of hell resting by a forgotten stream in Santa Monica . . . Valentine's Day in Los Angeles: listening to *Planet Waves* in Westwood, a rose bush scratching the window through which laughs early morning sunlight . . .

Our PSA Boeing 727 flew low over the Forum—the prodigious black parking-lot (a few cars, and the two FM Productions trucks) and the Forum itself, thrusting up like an out-take from *Fantasia* . . . A few miles in the distance was Malibu, where J. Paul Getty's detailed re-creation of a Greek building to house a museum is raising a "controversy" (like stunts in films) . . . Windows in the smog and breadlines where castles are burning in expectation of Nathaniel West's locusts . . . Valentine: two Christian martyrs who died at the hands of Romans . . . Valentine's Day in Los Angeles . . . and the eerie, thoughtful ghosts of mystery writers remain silent as they walk . . .

The man who goes singing to death is the brother of the man who goes to death fighting. A song on the lips is worth a dagger in the hand. I take this song and make it mine. Do you know what the song hides? A dagger, an outcry.

—Elie Wiesel, <u>The Gate of the Forest</u>.

The Forum, 14 February, 8:45: The girl ushers (looking like tryouts for a roller-derby war) stand idly in the aisles in front of the stage, a few feet from the light-control consoles . . . I am sitting with some of Dylan's relatives from Minnesota—kind people, genuinely interested in the poetry of the young, the feelings of young Jews . . . Lakers/N.B.A. flags emblazon the Forum's wall behind the stage . . . the atmosphere is electric—those about the stage both tense and expectant . . . Some of Mr. Graham's technicians tell me they have to work until almost 5:00 tomorrow morning, and their activity is rushed . . . Another aide mentions how Dylan was pleased with the reception in Oakland. And Los Angeles? The artists feel very fulfilled. The concert Wednesday night, 13 February: they had given everything they could, but one could sense an underly-

ing current of further expectation . . . During the concert this afternoon the current became more tangible, and now, thousands of faces appear for the third and last concert . . . The main floor is dotted with familiar figures—Warren Beatty, Carole King, among others . . .

9:20: Robert Hilburn of the *Los Angeles Times*, somewhat overjoyed; he attended the small gathering after this afternoon's concert in the Forum Club, organized by Bill Graham for members of the road crew . . . there was a belly dancer, a trio singing (with an accordion and two violins), and a wooden, guitar-shaped plaque for Dylan and each member of The Band, signed by Graham and the roadies . . .

9:23: Mr. Graham coming to the microphones . . . "This is our last concert, so we'll wait about five minutes" . . . He pauses for a moment, his face tired but creased with smiles . . .

9:35: Suddenly the lights are out . . . Rick Danko, then Robbie Robertson, followed by Garth Hudson, Richard Manuel, and, with a big smile, Dylan . . . Stands still for a moment . . . Raises both hands, the applause and the cheers and screams and everything rushing up at him . . . leans into his microphone . . . "Glad to be here!" . . . Sparklers go off in the audience . . . Jack Elliott and Neil Young, Ringo Starr and Joan Baez are pointed out by some nearby people with binoculars . . .

The Band begins a fast, energetic beat . . . Fender whispering pains . . . audience ecstatic . . . "RAINY DAY WOMEN" . . . whistles and stamping on first notes . . . "ev'ry body *must* get *stoned*!" . . . He breaks a string, but ignores it . . . Dylan widens his eyes in laughter . . . his face, streaming with perspiration . . . "you should be *made* to wear tele-*phones*!" . . . 10:02 . . . stands, bows, looking totally drained . . . departs . . .

The Zohar asks what a covenant with God is, what is meant in hearing the Voice—when that Voice is reflected in one's own hopes and aspirations, in the passions and empathies of a poet. The mystics said a covenant was like a dream. "A dream that is not remembered might as well not have been dreamt, and therefore a dream forgotten and gone from mind is never fulfilled."

Dylan is obviously excited . . . "Hey! Mister Tambourine Man!" . . . The audience is on its feet, as Dylan's voice—slow and soft—weaves with echoes of Yiddish proverbs and folklore . . . "into my parade . . . foggy ruins of time" . . . The Jewish soul yearns to dance, to sing; finding time to remember, to contemplate . . . Tears from the beauty of Dylan's awesome visions . . . Dylan starts to take off his guitar for the break, but Rick and Robbie rush around him . . . he is surprised . . . smiles . . . Then . . . "KNOCKIN' ON HEAVEN'S DOOR" . . . "*sick* and *tired* of this war!" . . . the melodiousness of the heart, the desire for freedom, the kiss of death . . .

We fill ourselves with *marirut*, living sadness; with *atzvut*, dead sadness. How is one to differentiate? The Ba'al Shem Tov, the founder of that mystical movement of Eastern European Jewry known as Hasidism, said that one is to look closely at another person after one has wept. One is to ask: "Do I hate this person, or do I love this person?" Living sadness is the ability to recognize that, even if one is engulfed in sorrow, another individual is also of the likeness of the divine. *Atzvut* is like what Dylan in "MR. TAMBOURINE MAN" calls "crazy sorrow." After weeping, one is unable to discern the beauty in the Creation because of the deadening sadness of self-inflicted sorrow.

10:58: Lights dim twice . . . Mr. Graham appears . . . "This is the last of forty, and there are some nice people left in this country, thank God. As soon as everyone is seated, we'd like to begin the second half" . . . Lights darkening . . .

Dylan, with a smile, walks slowly up on stage . . . bows . . . his acoustic guitar immediately echoes throughout the Forum . . . "She's got everything she needs" . . . "SHE BELONGS TO ME" . . . Dylan's harmonica weeping and inviting . . . "The Law *can't* touch her at all" . . . With a soft voice, almost drowned out by the immediate thunder of voices and applause . . . "THE TIMES THEY ARE A-CHANGING" . . . Inflections in the voice . . . He begins to sing louder and louder, urgently, raging . . . "rattle your *walls*" . . . Raises his left hand to those behind him . . .

"JUST LIKE A WOMAN" . . . lamentation . . . As David Meltzer has said to me: "The flow opening. The door. The window. Everything a passageway" . . . "she wakes . . . she breaks" . . . Dylan's guitar throbs (a word I've overworked, but what other adjective is there when, each verse, the guitar seems to quicken or slow itself?) . . . "I was hun-*gry* and *it* was *your* world" . . . The reminder of fragility, and, like a cantor, the harmonica bobs and sings . . . he bows . . . drinks from his cup . . . amidst a roaring standing ovation . . . "GATES OF EDEN" . . . The biblical images avalanche upon the soul . . . harmonizing with song . . . "promises of paradise" . . . Reality's contradictions . . . there are no sins inside the gates —while, outside . . . "there are no truths" . . . "I can *make* it!" . . . Smiling, then he grows serious . . . "*death's honesty*" . . . 11:30 . . . Bows to all . . . raises his guitar and harmonica . . . He is tired, but happy . . .

STEVE EPENETER

Rabbi Simeon said: "When God decided to create the world, He first produced the flame of a scintillating lamp. He blew spark against spark, causing darkness and fire, and produced from the recesses of the abyss a certain drop which He joined with the flame, and from the two He created the world. The flame ascended and encircled itself with the Left, and the drop ascended and encircled itself with the Right. They then crossed and changed places, going up and down alternately until they were closely interlocked, and there issued from between them a full wind. Then those two sides were made one, and the wind was set between them and they were entwined with one another, and so there was harmony above and harmony below; the grade was firmly established. —from the Zohar.

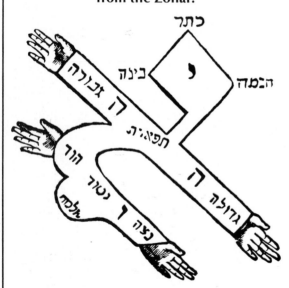

12:12: "On behalf of The Band and myself, good night!" . . . Pandemonium on stage . . . Bill Graham being carried around, being shot at with squirt guns . . . He almost faints with laughter when someone dumps a bucket of water on his head . . .

The various lighting and sound technicians have gone to bed, the music equipment on its way home. A rainbow kiss of light on the horizon announces that another day is beginning . . . The Forum Club, after the final concert, sandwiched with people . . . Dylan and Robbie Robertson . . . Cher Bono . . . David Crosby . . . Bill Graham . . .

Mr. and Mrs. Dylan left this after-concert gathering a little over two hours after it began. Dylan, alone, searched out the road crew and technicians who were packing equipment, and thanked each individually for their work during the tour. Bruce Byall, who directed the lighting during the concerts, was impressed by Dylan's warm gesture of gratitude; he, like all of the crew, felt that the tour had been a transcendental experience.

Two hours later, at the Beverly Wilshire hotel, a small gathering: Mr. and Mrs. Dylan, Robbie, David Blue, Lou Kemp, David Geffen, and others. Who can hope to capture in memory all of the textures of what was called TOUR 74 on the white/blue backstage passes? The words of the poet electrifying notes and hearts, his eyes laughing during the harmonica rhapsodies of "DON'T THINK TWICE," his voice, pleading and crying for compassion in "GATES OF EDEN" . . . The Band bouncing, or reincarnating the anguish of the winter of 1865 . . .

A Hasid once told me we are all stories—God likes to tell stories as well. And the Jewish soul of Bob Dylan, assailing our hearts with wedding songs, creating laments for those whose temples are leopard-skin pill-box hats, has said that men are friends when facing the Mystery.

Harmonization and reintegration transcend the turbulence of one-dimensionality. Bob Dylan is a vehicle of his own life. His path is his own and, sometimes, in the inner stillness, his footsteps mingle with ours. We reach for

the stars with one hand; with the other, we frantically touch our reality. The poet prays with his songs; he does not prophesy of probabilities and abstractions. Bob Dylan prays of Jewish possibilities, of human grief, of planet waves—of "life and life only," because life is all. We have discovered that we are messengers of the divine. In the oldest rabbinic commentary on Exodus, it is taught:

"Thy messengers, O God, are not like the messengers of human beings; for the messengers of human beings must needs return to those who send them before they can report. With Thy messengers, however, it is not so; but, Thou sendest forth lightnings . . ."

"May God bless and keep you always, Bob Dylan. *Aleichem shalom.*

Conclusion

Conclusion

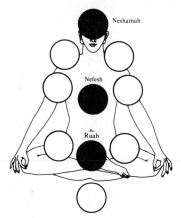

Neshamah

Nefesh

Ruah

"Dylan has told me," Theodore Bikel once said, "that Israel appears to be one of the few places left in the world where life has any meaning." In 1970, Dylan was invited to perform his poetry at an "Israel Birthday Be-In in Central Park." A student of Yeshiva University spoke to Dylan at this time, but Dylan decided not to appear, saying his appearance "would attract too many who had nothing to do with the cause." When the student started to explain the importance of the event, Dylan said, "I know, man, I *identify*."

In 1971 (May), Dylan arrived in Israel with his wife by El Al, staying at the Sharon Hotel, going to the beach, visiting with old friends, and writing. It was not Dylan's first visit to Israel, but the first in which journalists, somehow, discovered he was there (at the Wailing Wall). Dylan also visited a kibbutz, Neve Eitan, and upon returning to New York, he submitted an application with the Kibbutz Aliyah Desk in New York (his file, not open for inspection, is labelled: "Bob Dylan, guitar player"). Those in Israel who saw Mr. and Mrs. Dylan have told me that Mrs. Dylan was particularly moved by the profound faith of young

yeshiva students. But, when Neve Eitan received Dylan's application (for a one-year visit, to give him a chance to decide if he would permanently resettle), they were somewhat hesitant. There was some debate among kibbutz members: they were afraid of the publicity, of the kibbutz being overrun with visitors, of Dylan's privacy being invaded. They were also concerned about the ages of the Dylan children. Kibbutz children fall into specific educational age brackets and Dylan's children did not fit them. They finally sent Dylan a larger application in September 1972, but they never received a reply.

"Faith is the song of life," once wrote the Chief Rabbi of Israel (then Palestine, under British mandate), Rav Avraham Yitzhak Kuk. "Woe to him who wishes to denude life of the splendor of poetry." The songs/poems of Dylan are prayers—for redemption (*teshuvah*) in an age beset by *tohu* (chaos), the extant tribulations of lost souls.

The ungraspable hell which was the Holocaust has united the Jew with his soul. To survive, and to describe the joys and trials of such survival, is at the apex of Dylan's visions; visions which echo, reformulate, retell the profoundest les-

sons to be learned from those other poets, the Hasidim. Those who heard the Voice of Sinai have not forgotten the cries of the six million. Bob Dylan is a witness to an existence in which he, a Jew, must survive, and in surviving, share the paradoxes.

In his very first chapter, Ezekiel tells us: "The heavens were opened, and I saw visions of God." The rabbis of the Talmud believed that Ezekiel's visions, however transformative, could not parallel what the Jews *saw* at the Red Sea (*Mekilta de Rabbi Ismael*, ed. J. Z. Lauterbach).

Ezekiel (and all other Jewish prophets and poets) saw *visions* of the divine; but, they did not see the countenance of the *Source* itself. Even the maidservant present at the Red Sea saw what no other poet has since seen.

The rabbinic comment on Ezekiel is important if one is to grasp the tapestry I, a religious Jew, have approached Dylan

with in the previous pages. Throughout Jewish history, particularly with the Jewish mystics of the Middle Ages (and, in our time, with Rav Avraham Yitzhak Kuk, the early twentieth-century kabbalist, of blessed memory), poets of Israel have had to confront events which, seemingly, forever changed the responses of

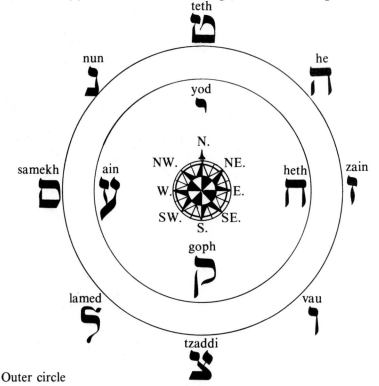

Outer circle

the core of Judaism to history. There-
after, poet mystics, through song and
prayer, strove to sense the radical
movements of their history, even if the
Presence remained dim. The theme of
all of Bob Dylan's mystic poetry is God's
presence in our existence—not a myth-
ological but an actual appeal to Him. In
his works, we understand while there
may be wicked messengers, while man
may worship desolation angels, God
Himself acts in man's life.

The Jew, especially Bob Dylan, cannot
deny He whose Presence seems absent.
Revelation, Emil Fackenheim has said,
"has a built-in content if only because it
is revelation—because it is not an ineffable Presence in man which dissolves
him, but rather a Presence speaking to
man which singles him out for response.
Hence all Jewish (believing) openness
to the future is a structured openness,
not an empty one, if only because it is an
openness which listens and responds,

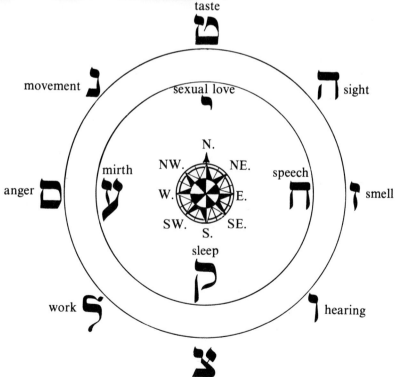

Inner circle

works and waits."

Throughout the 1974 North American tour, Bob Dylan provided us an access through his choice of songs (all dealing with the soul's struggle against spiritual obliteration), a time-warp by which the past-becomes-present. Bob Dylan presents, in his poetry, what Martin Buber called an "abiding astonishment," an awe of the Mystery, of events in his soul which provide him with a "glimpse of the sphere in which a sole power, not restricted by another, is at work."

Writes Bob Dylan in *Tarantula*: "you pray be to be righteous."

Planet Waves

Planet Waves

The language of music is letters
The music of poetry is letters
      —David Meltzer.

Hebrew letters on the wall
      —Bob Dylan, *Planet Waves.*

During our conversation at Chicago Stadium, the afternoon of 3 January 1974, amidst the hurried preparations for that evening's opening concert, Dylan's eyes watched the cables being laid, the piano being tuned. The bright spotlights illuminated the stage area as we sat down upon the brown couch which, for most of the tour, would rest behind the piano.

"I've got a new record coming out any day," Dylan said. "*Planet Waves*, on Elektra-Asylum."

"So soon?" I asked. "The newspaper reports have been rather contradictory about it. I assume you've decided against a label of your own?"

"Yes. I've carried the songs with me for a year now, and I'd be interested in what you'll have to say."

Planet Waves—with Dylan's superb cover painting of three people (one with what appears to be an anchor on the forehead), and two sentences on each side of the figures: "Moonglow" and "Cast-Iron Songs & Torch

Ballads"—appeared a few days later. However, it was not until 27 January, in New York City, that I was finally able to sit alone and listen to the album. Several hearings later, I gathered my notes and, at one sitting, wrote the review of *Planet Waves* which, in April, appeared in *Fusion*, the prestigious magazine of rock criticism edited by Robert Somma. On 3 February, in Bloomington, a photocopy of the review manuscript was given to Bill Graham, and on 4 February, in St. Louis, Dylan shared with me his feelings about it.

"I like the clarity of your views," he began, after saying "No, no, of course not," when I asked if anything I had written had offended him. He corrected two parts of the manuscript: one of the corrections was concerning "DIRGE." I had guessed that it was Richard Manuel on the piano. It was Dylan.

I again repeated to Dylan what I had written to him in a note accompanying the manuscript, that I sensed a tenacious spiritual reaching on his part in the songs. "Hoping," I said, "you'll be able to do 'DIRGE' at a forthcoming concert."

"There's a lot of material I wish I could do," he said. "The problem is where to fit it in." In a sense, I could see his point: "DIRGE," like "BALLAD OF A THIN MAN," is delivered with the piano as an important undercur-

---

With Leon Redbone and David Bromberg at the Mariposa Folk Festival, July 1972.

rent. The structure of the tour concerts re-
tained a certain flow, and introducing another Dylan poem with him at the piano
would interfere with the overall pattern.

"The songs on the album are important to
me," Dylan said.

"I tried to impart this in the review," I said.
"I think too many people are projecting neg-
ativism at you again. What you do is create
visions with music and words. It reminds me
too much of 1965, when people were trying
to dictate your poetic directions."

"Yeah, I know," Dylan said. "But what can
you do?"

Dylan's question is perhaps unanswerable. Scores of newspaper and magazine re-
views of concerts during the tour seemed to
ignore Bob Dylan the man, and illogically
bludgeon his work into an artifice. It appeared as though the purpose of the tour—
Dylan and The Band wanting to share, in as
relaxed a situation as possible, their music
and poetries—was lost in a plethora of criticism with no foundation.

On 17 July 1974, I interviewed Rob Fraboni,
engineer of *Planet Waves* and *Before The
Flood*, to gather his impressions.

SP: How did you feel, as an engineer,
about working with Bob Dylan in the studio?

RF: I liked it, I enjoyed working with him.
It was a special circumstance, and Dylan is a
special kind of artist. There was a special
kind of energy which, I think, was unique. It
was a really good thing to do.

SP: Can you describe how you first met
Dylan, the first day?

RF: It was 2 November. He walked in
with Robbie Robertson.

SP: Can you describe the sessions that
went into making *Planet Waves*?

RF: They came in for the first session on
2 November. Levon was out of town that
day. It was mostly to get a feel for the studio
and working together. "NEVER SAY GOODBYE"
came from that first day (with Richard Manuel on drums). On November 5, everyone
was there and we started recording the album. Usually three or four takes per song,
sometimes less. The arrangement and feel
would often change from take to take of the
same song. There were four or five versions

of "FOREVER YOUNG," for example (one version was acoustic, another had Garth Hudson's accordion), though only two of those
came from the same day. We worked hard.
Bob was the driving force, he kept the mo-
mentum up. He works really well with
The Band. The spontaneity of the sessions
showed me in another light what good musicians they are. Communication was good
. . . Since the album was recorded "live" in
the studio with Bob singing and everyone
playing, it was especially nice from my end
hearing the songs in their complete form first
time through. Much of the music really
moved me, Steve, and it moved them as well.
"FOREVER YOUNG" is a good example of that.
There were many. When recording "WED-
DING SONG," only myself, Bob, and a friend
of Bob's were in the studio (Lou Kemp).
With "DIRGE," only Robbie, Bob, and myself.
Those two songs especially impressed me.
They happened very quickly and very strong.
High impact.

SP: What were the noises, the clicking
sounds, one hears on the last half of
"WEDDING SONG"?

RF: It was a first take. Those are the but-
tons on his jacket hitting the body of the
guitar. I was adjusting the microphones, and
getting a sound in the booth, and Bob said,
"Let's roll it." I did and the song was done. I
believe it was one of the first times he had
played it.

SP: Did Dylan discuss with you his concept of what *Planet Waves* was about?

RF: No. The songs just happened. It was
very spontaneous. Bob is often quiet, saying
only what he needs to say.

SP: What went into *Before The Flood*?
How did you select the songs from the concerts of the tour?

RF: Each person that sang chose his own
performances. It was difficult because it was
live and mixing took longer than a studio
album.

ב

The Sessions for *Planet Waves* began on Friday, 5 November 1973,
continued on 6 November, then
finished on 9 November after a

two-day break. The album was recorded at the Village Recorder's Studio B, conceived by Rob Fraboni and designed by George Augspurger. Almost twenty-eight microphones were used, seven alone for Garth Hudson's Lowrey organ (with a Leslie on each of the two keyboards). Garth sometimes played the Lowrey and a Hammond organ simultaneously. There was no overdubbing. When Dylan "starts playing," Fraboni told Gary D. Davis of *Recording Engineer/Producer* (March-April 1974),

As a freshman in High School, Hibbing, Minnesota.

"there's nothing else happening but that, as far as he's concerned. I don't think I've seen anyone who performs with such conviction."

Before going to the Recorder, Dylan spent almost three weeks alone in New York, writing the songs ("FOREVER YOUNG" began germinating three years before the album). The final song recorded was the piano version of "DIRGE" (there is an out-take with Dylan on acoustic guitar). Fraboni, his assistant, Nat Jeffrey, and Robbie Robertson, were mixing songs while Dylan, in the studio, was playing the piano. He came in and

said to Fraboni: "I'd like to try 'DIRGE' on the piano." This first take was used for the album. Dylan "wanted certain types of sounds" during the sessions, Fraboni told Gary D. Davis. "He wanted a kind of barroom sound from the piano on 'DIRGE' rather than a majestic sound . . . Once we got into doing them, we mixed the whole album in about three or four days. But then we spent more time than it took to record or mix just to sequence the record. Bob wanted to *live* with a few different sequences, until he found one that was just right."

For "DIRGE" only, Dylan used a "windscreen," which prevents popping into the microphones. The piano itself was almost totally uncovered, but Dylan's intensity of singing forced Fraboni to use RE 15 microphones, pointing toward the back of the piano (rather than the hammers). "As far as (noise) leakage went," Fraboni told Davis, "it was really excellent. Plus, as I said, he wanted a more 'far away' sound for that number."

Mr. Fraboni later gave me the following credits for the tour album, *Before The Flood*, which were not printed on the jacket itself.

BEFORE THE FLOOD

Side One:
Most Likely You Go Your Way: 14 February (evening).
Lay Lady Lay: 13 February (evening).
Rainy Day Women: 13 February (evening).
Knockin' On Heaven's Door: Madison Square Garden, 30 January.
It Ain't Me, Babe: 14 February (evening).
Ballad Of A Thin Man: 14 February (afternoon).

Side Two:
Up On Cripple Creek: 14 February (evening).
I Shall Be Released: 14 February (afternoon).
Endless Highway: 14 February (evening).
Dixie: 14 February (evening).
Stage Fright: 14 February (evening).

Side Three:
Don't Think Twice: 14 February (evening).
Just Like A Woman: 14 February (evening).
It's Alright, Ma: 14 February (evening).
The Shape I'm In: 14 February (afternoon).

When You Awake: 14 February (evening).
The Weight: 13 February (evening).

　　Side Four:
All Along The Watchtower: 14 February (afternoon).
Highway 61 Revisited: 14 February (evening).
Like A Rolling Stone: 13 February (evening).
Blowin' In The Wind: a splice of 13 February (evening) and 14 February (afternoon).

ג

Cries, hurried whispers, laughter in an autumn wind, standing on edges of threshold experiences, we ask ourselves of reality's meaning. We ask questions—not knowing to whom we direct questions. We respond with pathos to the idea that, in order to draw our shadows near to the Mystery, we must "be"—not knowing what it is to "be." Our ideas of man/woman, humanity/Mystery appear lost when, in night skies, chaos is promulgated by television's metallically arthritic fingers, faraway sea-shell sounds behind closed curtains and squinted, moon-glow windows. We search for God in corridors. Long after midnight, with hands extended over hearthfire and coincidence, we discover that God is in search of man, calling out through the lights within, through planet waves.

"The fate of the world," say the Jewish mystics, "depends upon the mystery."[1]

Poets are mystics. Holding trembling ideas in nervous hands, poets tell us in songs and psalms that the mystery of the Mystery is unavoidable. The child's smile, a woman's loving glance, cannot be eradicated by neon Molochs.

We draw circles and stars of David upon the tree of life/light which is the soul. Opening eyes and ears, we see reflections of the light which is the Voice, the river. The river . . . defeated flowers, Brides of *bereshit*, of Creation, echoes of the All. "*Ha' eloha kol nimtza, v'ein kol nimtza Ha'eloha*," wrote the famous medieval mystic, Yitzhak Luria, of blessed memory. His words mean: "God is all that is found (that which is), but all that is found is not God."[2]

The ancient Rabbis tell us that YHWH desires not words, but the heart, not an eclipse of the soul, a withering of the tree, but apprehension of *orot*, Lights. Like a modern reincarnation of Isaac, we learn that the Breath, moving with locust intensity, is poetry; reminders that while the spirit has a home, the "home" of the ineffable Mystery is in the poet's eyes. Poetry—embellished with Robbie Robertson's mathematical guitar; the hymnlike organ of Garth Hudson; the mandolin and drums of Levon Helm; the wild mountain thymes of Richard Manuel's piano; Rick Danko's bass and haunting violin—is the Ineffable's search for man. The response, the light reflected into medicine for melancholia, of dream, of love, is to be found with Bob Dylan, a song of Imagination. Sound, words, notes—planet waves, combined in fusion chambers of mind and

Paris, May 1966.

RONALD SWEERING

1. *Sefer ha-Zohar*, trans. Maurice Simon *et. al.* 5 vols. (London: Soncino Press, 1931–1934), III: 128a.

2. Yitzhak Luria, quoted by Moses Cordovero, *Sefer Aleymah Rabbati* (Broday: 1881), p. 24d.

soul—telling us with dirgelike mystic insights, that YHWH is all reality, but all reality is not YHWH; that life without love is not life, but suffocation and death.

ד

"**W**e sensed each other," Dylan observes in his jacket notes, "beneath the mask, pitched a tent in the street & joined the traveling circus . . ." We watched the spiritually blind trying to drink a glass, a grail, with shaking hands, watched "thrashing clowns." Existence, for a time, became surreal; like the poems of the Russian Jew, Osip Mandelstam, our souls can become entangled in acrobatics and indifference. Looking at a broken mirror in a forgotten attic, the thrashing clown wears tattered dreams. With face painted by those who would deny life, deny love, the clown is the poet's conscience. He prays for the coming of the Messiah, slips paper into the Wailing Wall, simultaneously asking us if the Messiah's delay is, per-

Los Angeles, December 1965.

haps, rooted in the Messiah's shame. The clown thrashes, and the spectators gather in circles with nails and fiberglass crosses. Dreams of crucifiction flicker like torch light upon their faces, and they are angered, years later, when the poet refuses to die, refuses to be a martyr for their anti-spirituality.

The foundation for love, says one Talmudic rabbi, is the ability to refuse others' selfishness, that love cannot exist on a material foundation.[3] The poet, now on tour, stands in blue lights in Chicago, in Philadelphia, in Hollywood, Florida, in Denver, in cities of cardboard and human cries. The river flows, and his Jewish soul becomes like that of Jeremiah who, it is taught, tried for a time to withhold his spirituality. It became, instead, a "burning fire, shut up in my bones, and I weary myself to hold it in, but cannot" (Jeremiah 20:9). With harmonica voice and a soul enveloped in love, the poet watches the flowing river create planet waves. Yet he cannot forget the "thrashing clown." He cannot forget the "clown who cried in the alley" ("A HARD RAIN'S A-GONNA FALL"); the "saddened clown" one can become in one's own circus (jacket notes, *Joan Baez in Concert, Part 2*); the "ragged clown" ("MR. TAMBOURINE MAN"); "Cream Judge & the clown" (jacket notes, *Highway 61 Revisited*); "frowns on the jugglers and the clowns" ("LIKE A ROLLING STONE"); "all the clowns that you have commissioned" ("QUEEN JANE APPROXIMATELY"). The clown is the Joker who cries in the grip of confusion ("ALL ALONG THE WATCHTOWER").

ה

We create. We destroy. We have left, at times, shattered fragments for Bob Dylan. Can we question the pain that crosses his face? Can we ignore the tears? Can we ignore the joy, the love? The poet attempts to rebuild the temples man obliterates. Can we (must we?) demand of Bob Dylan that he rebuild the temples inside of *ourselves*?

---

3. (Babylonian Talmud), Pirke Avot, 5:19.

When Bob Dylan, with guitar and psalm, responds to his creation, to the Creation, he does so with pathos and sympathy, what the late Rabbi Abraham Joshua Heschel, of blessed memory, called apprehension of "divine possibility."[4] The concerns of Bob Dylan, his sympathetic pathos and mythopoeic visions, are with Life—and spiritual death as well. There exist no answers, but only Mystery; light and breath, darkness and silence. This pathos moves the poet. "It breaks out in him," wrote Heschel, "like a storm in the soul, overwhelming his inner life, his thoughts, feelings, wishes, and hopes. It takes possession of his heart and mind, giving him the courage to act against the world."[5]

Acting against the world: warning that "storm clouds" howl and attack one's door ("THE MAN IN ME"), produce poetic children of darkness, *blonde on blondes*, chaos. The world sleeps in pizza dreams and apathetic seizures. The poet screams out in d-minor, augmented with sight and touch. When we are indifferent even to the suffering of one person, the poet knows (and unhesitatingly tells us) that we are guilty of a spiritual crime. His kabbalah, his received wisdom, become our text(s). The poet can *never* be our conscience, although many have projected their fantasies of martyrdom upon all poets, and Bob Dylan in particular. The people who fail to listen to the Voice behind the poet's voice tenaciously insist that he be a "wicked messenger" ("THE WICKED MESSENGER"). But, it has been said that "A wicked messenger falleth into evil / But a faithful ambassador is health (Proverbs 13:17).

A faithful ambassador is health. His dreams, his visions, may cause both joy and frightening pain. He never conquers the mind with visions of Johanna, but will redirect the mind. And can it be argued that, for twelve years, such a redirector of emotions, an ambassador of spiritual health, has been Bob Dylan? To again quote Rabbi Heschel:

"The heaven's have no voice; the glory is inaudible. And it is the task of man to reveal what is concealed; to *be* the voice of glory, to sing its silence, to utter, to speak, what is in the heart of all things. The glory is here—invisible and silent. Man is the voice; his task is to be the song."[6]

ר

Rabbi Bahya ben-Asher, of blessed memory, enumerated that the numerical value of the Hebrew word *shirah* (song) is equal to that of *tefillah* (prayer).[7] *Planet Waves* is thus Bob Dylan's public prayer of joy and lamentation. His poems are dialogues with a *Thou*, not monologues with an *I*. His songs are both silence in the face of the mystery which is God, and also litany. Silence—the realization (as in "FATHER OF NIGHT") that All is beyond language. Litany—the further realization that the face of indescribable mystery (of love for children, for wife, for God) *is* the source of poetry/prayer. In setting love to poetry, we are safeguarding love. "Song opens a window to the secret places of the soul," says a Hasidic proverb I have heard. So does lack of love close the windows, the gates. At Mount Sinai, Moses heard the words *and* the silences between the letters. It snowed the year Daniel had his visions, one Jewish poet (Joel Rosenberg) has said. The trees bend under white burdens, and shadows cower. Birds with translucent wings hover over Desolation Row. Watching the River flow, Dylan's prayers fall upon our ears.

ר

Poetry/prayer is the language of Bob Dylan's soul. Poetry/prayer reveals that the *word* itself has movement, promise of action, memory of voices in search of faces. Words reflect the divine. Music is the language of the Ineffable, *histapkhuth hanefesh*, the

---

4. Abraham Joshua Heschel, *Between God and Man: An Interpretation of Judaism*, ed. Fritz A. Rothschild (New York: The Free Press, 1965), p. 124.

5. *Ibid.*, p. 125.

6. A. J. Heschel, "The Vocation of the Cantor," *Conservative Judaism*, Winter 1958.

7. Rabbi Bahya ben-Asher, Commentary on Numbers 21:19.

heart's outpouring of dreams and hopes. "The Lord made this world," teach the Jewish kabbalists of the twelfth-century *Sefer ha-Zohar*, "corresponding to the world above, and everything which is above has its counterpart below . . . and yet they all constitute a unity."[8]

Bob Dylan's struggle with chaos has been dialectical. The Jew, particularly since the Holocaust, is a survivor. The flames of Auschwitz are bent and bludgeoned; from destruction emanates a "new morning." Rather than extinguishing ourselves, we learn to see "the lights surrounding" the heart ("FOREVER YOUNG"). "The spirit of man is the lamp of the Lord / Searching all the inward parts" (Proverbs 20:27). With our inner breath, *nefesh*, we wipe the frost from spiritual windows, and extend our vision within. The lights surrounding us, Dylan has said, shine from "the west unto the east" ("I SHALL BE RELEASED"). Like some Jewish Gilgamesh, we watch memories exhale rattling lungs and die. Afraid to die, we search for love, for islands of immortality, which tell us, in riddles of pain and laughter, that there is no "secret" of existence, only Mystery. In winter winds—be they of Central Park or in Duluth—we contort our lips in questions, in answers, creating within mirrors for light, planet waves, dirges to startle sinning angels.

"Run your fingers down my spine / And bring me a touch of bliss," Dylan calls out in "ON A NIGHT LIKE THIS." He calls for the "four winds" to blow (similar to "BALLAD OF HOLLIS BROWN"—"seven breezes") around his "cabin door." We transform chaos which is, in actuality, ourselves. Before, the chaos was a torment for Bob Dylan. The fingers tied themselves in crippling knots ("JUST LIKE TOM THUMB'S BLUES") and became instruments of destruction: "your fingers goin' up my sleeve" ("SHE'S YOUR LOVER NOW"). The winds, too, raged against the soul's doors like "storm clouds" ("THE MAN IN ME"), refusing to give answers "blowin' in the wind"; while "in the wilderness / a cold coyote calls," and the air is punctured by seven winds ("BALLAD OF HOLLIS BROWN")—which,

in time, become a howling wind ("ALL ALONG THE WATCHTOWER").

The "winds of changes" ("FOREVER YOUNG") are of many faces: "Let the four winds blow" ("ON A NIGHT LIKE THIS"); a "changing wind" ("TOUGH MAMA"); a "whirlwind" ("SOMETHING THERE IS ABOUT YOU"); and winds which tear at the heart ("BLOWIN' IN THE WIND," "BALLAD OF HOLLIS BROWN," and "THE MAN IN ME"). We sense, beneath the poet's denotations, that God Himself will "swoop down upon the wings of the wind" (Psalm 18:11). There are "Precious winds" ("GATES OF EDEN") which blow through our consciousness ("SUBTERRANEAN HOMESICK BLUES," "ALL ALONG THE WATCHTOWER," and "LOVE MINUS ZERO"). The wind is "the voice of a great rushing" (Ezekiel 3:12) a touching, an urging that we breathe in life and exhale our illusions, the "cyclone wind on a steam engine howler" ("LAST THOUGHTS ON WOODY GUTHRIE"), a wind which "blows hard" ("FAREWELL"). We must, said the poet long ago, turn our faces, "turn to the rain / And the wind" ("PERCY'S SONG"). "He makes winds his messengers," teaches a prayer for Yom Kippur.[9] And a tenth-century poet, R. Meshullam ben Kalonymus wrote: "Deliver them from howling tempests" (compare "howling" to how Dylan uses the symbol in "ALL ALONG THE WATCHTOWER").

In the Talmud (Sotah 31a), it is said: "Two disciples stood before Rabha. One told him: In my dream they taught us, 'Oh how abundant is Thy goodness, which Thou hast laid up for them that fear Thee, in the sight of the sons of men! (Psalm 31:20).' The other told him: In my dream they taught us,

> 'So that all those that take
> refuge in Thee rejoice,
> They shall ever shout for joy,
> And Thou shalt shelter them;
> Let them also that love Thy name
> exult in Thee.'
> —Psalm 5:12.

---

8. Zohar, II, 20a.

9. *Machzor Ha-Shalem L'Rosh Ha-Shanah V'Yom Kippur*, trans. Philip Birnbaum (New York: Hebrew Publishing Co., 1951), "Morning Service for Yom Kippur," p. 654.

Top: London, May 1966, and above: On the set of *Pat Garret and Billy the Kid*, late 1972.

"He said to them: You are both perfectly righteous men, the one from love, the other from fear."

We search for the causal nexus in our hearts, for the Mystery which shimmers behind our words, for the fact of our existence. After experiential encounters with God, we then schematize with ideational after-effects. The poet in *Planet Waves* cannot teach (describe) the Mystery, the ineffable. His words, however, can awaken in one a response to the poet's own awakening, the poet's response to the numinous. Thus we can say that *kodesh*, holiness, creates by its own essence dialogue, awe, and sometimes, fear.

Man must, said Rav Avraham Yitzhak Kuk, of blessed memory, break the chains of fear which would prevent mankind from discovering the divine. These chains, he insisted, would be like wicks for the fires of the awakened soul: "like fine threads of flax which are consumed by burning flames." Thus, there would occur a revolution in one's soul, forming a foundation from which we could see the lights within, the "lights surrounding you" ("FOREVER YOUNG"). In Rav Kuk's words, such a transformation of one's soul is a "sign that the light of the soul, in all of its aspects, is in the process of being rebuilt, and the light of a heavenly salvation proceeds to reveal itself in a host of golden sparks" (loosely translated from Kuk's *Orot haKodesh*). Man listens. He searches for truth. He calls out with planet waves, and is answered by the roaring wheels and lights of the *Shekhinah*. When he believes his cries to be unanswered (or unanswerable), then a "trembling distant voice, unclear" touches his soul ("IT'S ALRIGHT, MA"). We search for the soul in times of evaporation. But, God hears one's voice, is aware of "all them that call upon Him in truth" (Psalm 145:18). We discover truth ("FOREVER YOUNG"), that the highway to Him is mercy and truth (Psalm 25:10).

It is not the discovery of truth which is important for the Jewish poet in *Planet Waves*. Rather, the honest *search* for truth—with its reward and its dangers—is paramount. There is "frost on the window glass / With each new tender kiss," Dylan states in "ON A NIGHT LIKE THIS." Outside of the soul, chaos extends frigid fingers: "The windows are filled with frost" ("IT TAKES A LOT TO LAUGH, IT TAKES A TRAIN TO CRY"). The windows of the soul are a pathway for consciousness, and the poet dares us to open the shades: "CAN YOU PLEASE CRAWL OUT YOUR WINDOW" (released as a single in 1965, there are two existing out-takes of this formidably evocative poem); "I put my fingers against the glass" ("I DREAMED I SAW ST. AUGUSTINE"). If we cannot—if we enslave ourselves to repetition, then truth is only a hope. "Build a fire," Dylan pleads in "ON A NIGHT LIKE THIS." A fire over which we can warm our hearts and souls, rather than allow the flames to char our eyes: "Crying like a fire" ("IT'S ALL OVER NOW, BABY BLUE"); or to forget "The Holy Kiss that's supposed to last eternity" ("LOVE IS JUST A FOUR-LETTER WORD"; Dylan again uses "eternity" in "WEDDING SONG").

Thus love is a reality which "many waters cannot quench, neither can floods drown it" (Song of Songs 8:7). In the Talmud, it is said that Moses and Miriam died by a holy kiss.[10]

In "GOING GOING GONE," a compelling evocation of pain, Dylan is "closing the book / On the pages of the text." Earlier, with "TOO MUCH OF NOTHING," the text (of the past) loomed with letters flaming on the pages: "It's all been written in the book." We stand, said Martin Buber, on the edge; if pushed, we can see ourselves die. If we stand back, we can see ourselves live. Highway 61 becomes a mirage; with thematic determination we can, says Dylan, live "on the edge"; but stepping back is a necessity, "before I get to the ledge."

ה

"TOUGH MAMA" (like "TELL ME, MAMA," of which several taped versions from the 1966 European tour exist) is a pounding, yet joyous/paradoxical poem. (Its presentation, at the two opening concerts in Chicago, 3 and 4 January, brought applause and smiles.) Existence is accentuated with theomorphic laughter, and like S. Y. Agnon and Elie Wiesel, Dylan's laughter also precipitates thoughtfulness. "I'm goin' down to the river," he says. The river . . . of life. In an untitled poem (on tape, 1962/1963), Dylan has said: "The autumn wind keeps blowin' / Tryin' to make that river scream." We knock on heaven's door, and "as the sun goes down / the doors

of the river are open" (liner notes, *Another Side of Bob Dylan*). "I'm going down to the river" . . .

> I gazed in the river's mirror
> And watched its winding strum.
> The water smooth ran like a hymn
> And like a heart did strum.
> —from "LAY DOWN YOUR
> WEARY TUNE"

The river . . . of existence.

"I can't see my reflection (an image appearing in "I SHALL BE RELEASED") in the waters," Dylan has lamented. "I can't speak the sounds that show no pain" ("TOMORROW IS A LONG TIME"; note similar usage of "pain" as it appears in "JUST LIKE A WOMAN"). The Talmud (Baba Qama 17a) has compared the Torah to the rushing of waters, and the Hasidim have spoken of the waters of the "divine soul." Existence itself is at stake for the poet; in singing for joy, we can sense the fear and trembling behind Dylan's words. The Ba'al Shem Tov once said that, when someone is drowning in a river, and his fear is manic as he tries to rescue himself from the waters, those who try to rescue the drowning man do not stand about and laugh among themselves.

So, then, said the Ba'al Shem Tov, when a man prays (and is not Dylan's work a prayer?), we should withhold judgment if he seems hysterical or enraged, because the man who prays/sings his poetry is trying to rescue his soul from the river's waters. "Say of God," it is said in the morning prayers for Yom Kippur, "His path is over deep waters; He causes rain (compare "FATHER OF NIGHT") to drop from the skies (note "IT'S ALL OVER NOW BABY BLUE" in reference to "sky"); morning and evening ("MR. TAMBOURINE MAN": "evening's empire"), his Oneness is proclaimed at the gates of crowded synagogues" (i.e. at "gates of Eden" and "heaven's door").

There are "fields where the flowers are," which, at one time, were held by fishermen ("DESOLATION ROW"), and his love "laughs like the flowers" ("LOVE MINUS ZERO/NO LIMIT"). And the Tough Mama, is she not both

---

10. (Babylonian Talmud), Baba Batra 17a.

Lilith (that woman of Jewish legend who found Adam sanctimoniously strenuous) and the *Shekhinah*, the indwelling Presence? She is—now—a "silver angel," and a "Sweet Goddess, born of a blinding light" (note Dylan's mystical usage of "light" in "I SHALL BE RELEASED," "FOREVER YOUNG," and "ONE MORE NIGHT"), "and a changing wind" (note "wind" in "FOREVER YOUNG"). She bears the "badge of the lonesome road." Before, likewise, existence pointed to a "metal badge" ("GATES OF EDEN"), and a "badge out, laid off" ("SUBTERRANEAN HOMESICK BLUES"). Now "the world of illusion is at my door," and we yearn for refuge.

The *Shekhinah* has also been a "silver-studded phantom" ("GATES OF EDEN") and a "goddess of gloom" ("JUST LIKE TOM THUMB'S BLUES"). Existence is dualistic: "I stood alone up on the ridge," Dylan now says, "And all I did was watch." As people on a bridge, urging someone to jump, we can also urge our souls (and thus the souls of those who touch us through dialogue, to abandon a script meant for a near-blind gunfighter. We can hear Mr. Tambourine Man keeping time with David's harp, the River's strum; we can hear, as well, the cry of a child, the breath of a sleeping woman. We have, said the Jewish mystics, both man and woman within us. Turning (*teshuvah*) is circular, a nurturing or organismic thought. Must existence be "one more notch and four more aces" ("BILLY 4")? Must it be "time to carve another notch" ("TOUGH MAMA")? The "damp dirty prisons" ("A HARD RAIN'S A-GONNA FALL") are now, insists Dylan, "crumbling," and there is "no end in sight."

ℶ

It has been said: For Thou dost light my lamp; / The Lord my God doth lighten my darkness" (Psalm 18:29). It has been said by Bob Dylan: "Father of night, Father of day, / Father, who taketh the darkness away" ("FATHER OF NIGHT"). To create *tikkun*, reintegration, man must love. The *Shekhinah*, the Presence, lights the candle within our hearts.

The soul, the body, of man/woman, is a unity, said the Jewish mystics. The soul's vitality (*nefesh*) is a base of a candle, the dim light, invisible at one moment, flickering at another just within the range of vision. Unified, mankind is a flame, a reflection of Light. Is this not the core of both "HAZEL" and "SOMETHING THERE IS ABOUT YOU"?

We can, Dylan has said, not trust our brother/sister (inside leaf, *Writings and Drawings*); we can turn away, leading to our "fatal doom, / To wander off in shame" ("I AM A LONESOME HOBO"). Trust, dialogue, love—intertwined paths, highways, to *shalom*, completeness. We can ask for the "touch of your love" ("HAZEL"), or we can "pretend that we never have touched" ("I DON'T BELIEVE YOU"); or worse—"Rasputin he's so dignified, / He touched the back of her neck and he died" ("I WANNA BE YOUR LOVER").

In nights when silence is a welcomed companion, our eyes discern "stardust in your eye" ("HAZEL"). In days when violence erupts in an I-It existence, "she had bullets in her eyes, and they fire" ("I WANNA BE YOUR LOVER"). We can struggle; we can die on a hilltop ("IT TAKES A LOT TO LAUGH, IT TAKES A TRAIN TO CRY"). And Hazel, standing beneath magnolia trees, will see that we are "up on a hill." Is the hill that of Sinai? When Hazel is absent, "it's just makin' me blinder." It is a day when a dark cloud appears ("KNOCKIN' ON HEAVEN'S DOOR"; in the tour version, the cloud became a train), when there is, in the soul of mankind, "gloominess" and "thick darkness" (Joel 2:2).

The darkness, the eclipse of man, of love, the imperialism of the indifferent—these are the foci of the Jewish poet's visions. The darkness: "Statues made of match sticks" ("LOVE MINUS ZERO/NO LIMIT"). The light: "match-book songs" ("SAD-EYED LADY OF THE LOWLANDS"); "Something there is about you / That strikes a match in me." Desolation Row's Phantom of the Opera is now a ripple in a planet wave: "phantoms of my youth." And, in an earlier poem, Dylan wrote: "An' spit at strong with vomit words . . . T' be my voice an' tell my tale / An' help me fight my phantom brawl" (*Joan Baez in Concert, Part 2*, liner notes).

Mr. and Mrs. Dylan at the Mariposa Folk Festival, July 1962.

PHOTOGRAPHS BY ART USHERSON

The fragile state of truth needs consistent renewing: "brings back a long-forgotten truth" ("SOMETHING THERE IS ABOUT YOU"). The truth—ignoring man's definitions: "of war and peace the truth just twists" ("GATES OF EDEN"). The truth is an analogue for honesty—with one's self, with one's wife, with God.

> I could say that I'd be faithful
> I could say it in one sweet, easy breath
> But to you that would be cruelty
> And to me that surely would be death.

Honesty, like a candle, sheds illumination, mystic hammering against the "whirlwind." The fingers are no longer bound with knots, but hesitatingly touching: "Something there is about you / That I can't quite put my finger on."

"DIRGE," with Dylan's voice conjuring up the pain which culminates in self-honesty (augmented by the haunting keyboards of Dylan's piano), returns again and again to consciousness. A love watered with hypocrisy, with a "painted face" and a "suicide road" is an existence, hence, of "crazy faces" ("BILLY 4"), and of "suicide remarks" ("IT'S ALRIGHT, MA"). It is, moreover, an existence, faced by all Jews:

> And I felt that place within
> That hollow place where martyrs weep
> And angels play with sin.

The images, one discovers, cannot be forgotten—nor can they be ignored. We stand, again, not at the Sinai of the soul, but at the apex of chaos—where "mothers weep" ("I WANT YOU"), and where there are no "martyrs" ("I DREAMED I SAW ST. AUGUSTINE"). There are, in alleyways, "bread-crumb sins" ("GATES OF EDEN"). Love, to grow, to mature, must have a foundation. Without such a foundation, man deifies Halloween, stripping himself of his soul, blowing upon the flames of Auschwitz until the depths of hell extinguish our souls. "I paid the price of solitude," Dylan reminds us, "But at least I'm out of debt . . . The naked truth is still taboo / Whenever it can be seen."

"I've paid the price of solitude / But at least I'm out of debt," Dylan cries out, and his emphasis on "solitude" cannot be ignored. The concept of solitude as a vehicle with which one can obviate the vapid surrealism of modern life is not without foundation. Before recording *Planet Waves*, Dylan had read Gabriel Garcia Marquez's *One Hundred Years of Solitude*, a powerful evocation of thoughts and dream/reality. Marquez, like Bob Dylan in "DIRGE," is concerned with unities, of alabasters of hope—with solitude as the soul's luminosity, with encyclicals of essence and existence, of alone-ness, of joy and melancholia.

The Jewish mystics, particularly the Hasidim, are very aware of the path of *hitbodedut* (solitude). The Tzartkover Rabbi (David Moses, died 1903) was once observed by his followers as having seemingly failed to teach Torah for some time. When asked why, he looked at them for a long time, then said: "There are seventy ways of reciting Torah. One of them is through silence (or solitude)." Martin Buber, in *Ten Rungs: Hasidic Sayings*, has written: "When I look at the world, it sometimes seems to me as if every man were a tree in the wilderness (compare "tree" to "haunted, frightened trees in "MR. TAMBOURINE MAN"; and "wilderness" as it is used in "ALL ALONG THE WATCHTOWER"), and God had no one in his world save him alone, and he had none he could turn to, save God alone."[11]

The soul, said Dylan in "TOO MUCH OF NOTHING," may become engulfed in "fire"; it may, like a wandering specter of desire, forget the meaning of truth, that before the divine a "fire goeth" (Psalm 97:3). "A Jew who does not rejoice in the fact of his being a Jew is ungrateful toward heaven," Rabbi Abraham Joshua Heschel, of blessed memory, wrote. Such an existence "is a sign that he has failed to grasp the meaning of having been born a Jew. Even lowly merriment has its ultimate origin in holiness. The fire of evil can be better fought with flames of ecstasy than through fasting and mortification."[12]

---

11. Martin Buber, *Ten Rungs: Hasidic Sayings*, trans. Olga Marx (New York: Schocken Books, 1962), p. 18.

We have been, says Scripture, "chastised . . with whips . . . with scorpions" (First Kings 12:11). We become, says Dylan in "DIRGE," one who is "Acting out his folly / While his back is being whipped." And we "watch upon your scorpion" ("TEMPORARILY LIKE ACHILLES"), which attacks and mortally wounds the soul with illusions.

Our hearts, Dylan appears to warn, cannot endure a metamorphosis—becoming apparitions, clinging with desperate savagery to delusion, making the "naked truth" a "sin." The world becomes the dialectic of a "wicked messenger." "I saw under the sun ("foreign sun"; "GATES OF EDEN"), in the place of justice, that wickedness was there; and in the place of righteousness ("righteous"; "FOREVER YOUNG"), that wickedness was there" (Ecclesiastes 3:16). "God's absence is an illusion," Rabbi Heschel has written. "The senses deceive us into believing that God is nowhere to be found. The world lives by revealment and concealment . . . the Glory is everywhere, but with the palm of one hand upon our eyes, we obstruct our own view. To

a large degree, the darkness is due to a failure of experience. Our mind is obscured by the eclipse, not the sun. The soul is 'a part of God from above,' but man thinks he is all from below, all made of dust. Every man must think of himself as a stairway set on the ground, its top reaching heaven. It is within his power to affect what should happen in the upper worlds."[13]

An eleventh-century kabbalist and poet, R. Elijah ben Mordecai wrote: "The mighty champion Abraham discerned thy truth / In an age when all failed to know how to please thee."

"YOU ANGEL YOU," "NEVER SAY GOODBYE," and the awesome "WEDDING SONG," are, like the two versions of "FOREVER YOUNG," psalmic pleas and breath-taking reaffirmations. "And He hath put a new song in my mouth," the Psalmist teaches, "even praise unto our God" (Psalm 40:4). Said one Hasidic master, "(songs) are derived from a source of sanctity, from the Temple of Song." We yearn for a "strong foundation" ("FOREVER YOUNG"), and, out of the whirlwind, we can create such a foundation for the soul (Proverbs 10:25). As the wind sings through the mind, as rains dance and weep upon the roofs of our souls, we see a "twilight on the frozen lake" and "silence down below" ("NEVER SAY GOODBYE"). If, at one time, dreams were threatened with a guillotine ("IT'S ALRIGHT, MA"), now such dreams "are made of iron and steel / With a big bouquet of roses"; roses—carried by children, by all of us ("LOVE MINUS ZERO/NO LIMIT"). Finally, as the storm subsides, we stay forever young, composing wedding songs, rather than "breathe out violence" (Psalm 27:12).

"WEDDING SONG" is celebration, is joy intensified.

Once wrote Rabbi Heschel: "When we talk about the need for joy, says one of the

12. A. J. Heschel, *The Earth Is The Lord's and The Sabbath* (New York: Harper Torchbooks, 1966), p. 76.
13. A. J. Heschel, *A Passion For Truth* (New York: Farrar, Straus and Giroux, 1973), pp. 18–19.

great Hasidic masters, we do not mean the joy that comes from fulfilling the commandments; for the ability to feel such spontaneous joy is the privilege of illustrious souls, and one cannot expect it of every Jew. What we mean then is the banishment of sadness."[14]

"Love you more than madness," Dylan insists, more than "waves upon the sea." The poet now stands "silhouetted by the sea . . . With all memory and fate driven deep beneath the waves" ("MR. TAMBOURINE MAN"). We hear the whispering of the divine (see Isaiah 6:3); we hear, also, Job: "The earth is given into the hand of the wicked; He covereth the faces of the judges" (Job 9:24). We see, says Dylan in "WEDDING SONG," the "faces in the street." We see the lights of freedom, "With faces hidden" ("CHIMES OF FREEDOM"). We also see the face of chaos. "Get thee from me, take heed to thyself, see my face no more; for in the day thou seest my face thou shalt die" (Exodus 10:28).

Shadows flicker, and with tenacity, man struggles and shrieks against the lacunae that would erase his soul. The "Executioner's face," Dylan has said ("A HARD RAIN'S A-GON-NA FALL") is often hidden in the tentacles of mucilaginous *angst*. The victim, says the Jewish poet, is man's freedom: "His face was all grounded in the cold sidewalk floor" ("ONLY A HOBO"). Dylan bids farewell to faces, which, carved in pyramidal consciousness, become for him hieroglyphs: "Time traveled an' faces passed" (*Joan Baez in Concert, Part 2*, liner notes); "I had to rearrange their faces" ("DESOLATION ROW").

"I love you more than ever /And it binds me to the soul," Dylan enunciates. In the published version of "WEDDING SONG," the words are different: "Quenched my thirst and satisfied / The burning in my soul." (Compare the image of "thirst" to its usage in "THE BALLAD OF FRANKIE LEE AND JUDAS PRIEST," and the image of "burning" as it appears in "THE WICKED MESSENGER.") Binding to the soul, love is a covenant, both a wall against artificiality and a pathway to rejuvenation. The image of "binds" is important. For the Jewish mystics, the concept of *devekut* ("cleaving" or binding one's soul to

God) enabled one in solitude (*hitbodedut*) to integrate one's soul with the "upper" worlds. The Torah (Deuteronomy 13:5) provided the foundation: "and unto Him shall ye cleave." According to Isaac the Blind, such a binding of one's soul enables one "to harmonize one's thought with one's faith as though it cleaved to (the worlds) above . . ."[15] Another kabbalist, Meir ibn Gabbai, said: "And when it (the soul) reaches its source, it cleaves to the celestial light (Dylan's Jewish concept of *orot ha'kodesh*, the lights of holiness, is articulated in "I SHALL BE RELEASED") from which it derives and the two become one."[16]

Dylan's articulation of his own *devekut* cannot be ignored. Man seeks for the ascension of the soul. *Devekut*, in the words of Gershom Scholem, means "a constant being-with-God which is not dependent on death and life after death . . . *Devekut* is a value of contemplative, not of active life . . . A man might appear to be with other people, to talk to them, and, perhaps, even to participate in their activities, but in reality he is contemplating God."[17]

Devekut, binding, thus is a path and not an end-in-itself; rather, the Jewish poet shows one the multiplicity of such paths, which eventually lead to *yihud*, reintegration of one's soul. The poet removes the illusions and points one toward the actual content of one's visions; the immanence of God becomes present in one's binding.

Man reaches for higher stages of the soul, even though existence will, in a kabbalistic sense, bring one's consciousness to a lower stage. In the words of Pinhas of Koretz, of blessed memory, "the world is really God Himself, like the locust whose clothing is part of its own self."[18] (Note the similarity to Dylan's motif in "DAY OF THE LOCUSTS.")

---

14. *Ibid.*, p. 52.
15. quoted, Gershom Scholem, *Kabbalah* (New York: Quadrangle/The New York Times Book Co., 1974), p. 175.
16. quoted, *ibid.*
17. Gershom Scholem, *The Messianic Idea in Judaism: And Other Essays on Jewish Spirituality* (New York: Schocken Books, 1971), pp. 204-205.
18. quoted, *ibid.*, p. 225.

Man's ascension, however, is not anarchic, although his strength is tested. Existence, said one Hasidic master, is "a door which one opens with something which can break iron. Thus the ancients employed in meditation the *kavvanah* (intentions) suitable for each thing (i.e., each existential encounter). (But) now that we have no *kavvanah*, only the breaking of the heart will open (the door) to everything."[19] Another Hasidic master, Aaron of Starosselje, said: "Love of God and cleaving (*devekut*) to Him are unimaginable without the knowledge of His unity, Blessed be He."[20]

Our eyes have seen "rivers of tears" ("WENT TO SEE THE GYPSY"), those tears which "run down like a river" (Lamentations 2:18). Facing both the illusiveness of reality's dreams and dreams of reality, the willows do not bend, nor does love. The poet learns to love "more than madness, more than dreams upon the sea," learns to "say goodbye to haunted rooms and faces in the street" ("WEDDING SONG"). "And if there is eternity, / I'll love you there again." Eterni-ty—of the Holy Kiss ("LOVE IS JUST A FOUR-LETTER WORD"); of the museums of thoughts which try, even when beyond man's capacities, to institute courtrooms and put "infinity up on trial" ("VISIONS OF JOHANNA"). We look at our souls, seeing the Light, the planet waves, our "brothers of the flood" (liner notes).

ב

"There are those," Dylan says, "who worship loneliness," who create a manifold ambivalence to human suffering, an "age of fiber glass." Like a snowflake patterned on a cracked window, the Jewish soul rejects "flesh-colored Christs that glow in the dark"

---

19. R. Dov Baer, quoted from Joseph Weiss, "The *Kavvanoth* of Prayer in Early Hasidism," *The Journal of Jewish Studies*, IX (1958).

20. quoted, Louis Jacobs, *Seeker of Unity: The Life and Works of Aaron of Starosselje* (New York: Basic Books, 1966), p. 78.

Singing with Phil Ochs and Dave van Ronk at the benefit for Chile concert, May 1974.

BOB GRUEN

("IT'S ALRIGHT, MA"), rejects those who deny that there is nothing sacred, nothing which can hypnotize the soul's glance ("NOBODY BUT YOU," an unreleased song from the November 1973 sessions which resulted in *Planet Waves*). "Father of loneliness and pain, / Father of love and Father of rain," Dylan cries out. "I love you more than madness, more than dreams upon the sea," he now reminds us with "WEDDING SONG." "In the courtyards of the jester, hidden from the sun," we can lose ourselves. Courtyards— "The jacks and queens / Have forsaken the courtyard" ("FAREWELL ANGELINA"). Sacrificing the world, Dylan says, so that senses will die in the harmonics of wedding songs. We shut our "watery eyes," and then the "pangs of your sadness / Shall pass as your senses will rise" ("TO RAMONA"). We recite wedding songs, recite silence—thus reciting the calling of the divine to man.

"Woe to him who has no courtyard," says one rabbinic sage, "yet makes a gate for the same."[21] The gates of Eden, heaven's door— however one reaches, one must nurture one's soul with planet waves, with righteousness. It is written: "the righteous shall live by his faith" (Habakkuk 2:4); "O Lord, let me not be ashamed, for I have called upon Thee" (Psalm 31:18). Our illusions—"What's lost is lost . . . / What went down in the flood" ("WEDDING SONG"; the biblical image of flood is also used by Dylan in "DOWN IN THE FLOOD")—are illusions, syncretic "realities." Our realized reality is the binding, the listening to the melodies of solitude, recapitulation of the quotidianism of hope. He who understands *devekut*, the binding, said the Spanish kabbalist Isaac of Acre (fourteenth century), understands what it is when the soul "attains to loneliness . . . to the holy Spirit and to prophecy."[22] Being-with-God, being with one's lover—this is the spirit which Dylan utilizes as a vehicle for his thoughts.

"Mercy and truth are met together," says the Psalmist (85:11), "Righteousness and peace have kissed each other." The "winds of changes" ("FOREVER YOUNG") call out from the leaves of abandoned dreams; listening, the poet knows that the divine rides the

"wings of the wind" (Psalm 18:11). What is demanded of and by the Jewish poet in *Planet Waves* is truth. "Truth is inwardness," Rabbi Abraham Joshua Heschel, of blessed memory, tells us, "inwardness is authenticity, and authenticity is attained through intense, passionate inner action. Only integrity can save man and his faith."[23] "For there is not," it is written, "a righteous man upon the earth, that doeth good, and sinneth not" (Ecclesiastes 7:20). Even "angels play with sin" ("DIRGE"), and our soul's garments may be torn by darkness as they can be mended by light.

There are no conclusions, no answers; opening the windows of the soul with song, we hear (and gain) only premises, the intransigence of illusion, the self-perpetrating tensions of truth. The vortex of our vision must not be allowed to evolve into opaqueness; our soul is both the plane of anguish and the apex of joy. Our soul, said one sage, is "melting with secret sorrow" when we think of those martyred,[24] the *noleus voleus* of destruction and re-creation, estuaries of the soul binding its destiny to rejuvenation. Man prays for redemption from the seemingly endless avenues of spiritual repression. Abba Arika, a third-century Talmudic rabbi, suggested that God prayed as well: that "My mercy may suppress My anger, that My mercy may prevail over My other attributes, so that I may deal with My children in the attribute of mercy and on their behalf stop short of the limit of stern justice."[25] God prays. God weeps. God laughs—and the echoes wake us in the night and, sometimes, fill men with shame.

Seeking, we call out for the *raison d'être* for our tribulations. Calling out, many will project their hells upon the Jewish poet,

PRECEEDING PAGE: VERNON SHIBLA

21 quoted, A. J. Heschel, *A Passion For Truth*, p. 55.
22. quoted, Gershom Scholem, *Major Trends in Jewish Mysticism*, trans. George Lichtheim (New York: Schocken Books, third revised edition, 1961), p. 96.
23. A. J. Heschel, *A Passion For Truth*, p. 127.
24. unknown poet of Geonic period, quoted, Philip Birnbaum, *Machzor Ha-Shalem*, "Additional Service for Yom Kippur," p. 838.
25. (Babylonian Talmud), Berakot 7a.

who retreats into privacy, not sharing his discoveries. The *angst* of reality is our soul encountering in *Planet Waves* what Sören Kierkegaard called the "unconditional." Without existentially encountering the unconditional, he insisted, man would live but a life without spirit ("her sin is her lifelessness," said Dylan in "DESOLATION ROW"). It is no longer possible—after Auschwitz, after Buchenwald—for man to disbelieve. It is not man's duty "to remake the world at large" ("WEDDING SONG"). But man must ask questions of God: do You have a "free will"? Can we become *tzaddikim* and annul the heavenly decree which entails that You be eclipsed? We have been told that we are blessed with holiness, because—through humiliation, extermination, blood—You are holy (Leviticus 19:2). We slay not the innocent and righteous (Exodus 23:7) in our minds—even while the mothers of fallen sons share their tears, and watch the skies become exploding galaxies of bullets and songs. Implicit in faith is demand, is struggle. "My soul thirsteth for God, for the living God: 'When shall I come and appear before God?'" (Psalm 42:2). "Quenched my thirst," writes Dylan in the published version of "WEDDING SONG."

> For the enemy hath persecuted my soul;
> He hath crushed my life down to the
>   ground;
> He hath made me to dwell in dark
>   places, as those that have been
>   long dead.
> And my spirit fainteth within me;
> My heart within me is appalled.
>   —Psalm 143:3–4.

The poet listens. His tongue unleashes vision and sound. "An' I locked myself an' lost the key / An' let the symbols take their shape" (*Joan Baez in Concert, Part 2*, liner notes). The soul, says one prayer for Yom Kippur, the holiest day of the Jewish soul, "belongs to Thee."[26] If man does good, it is taught in the Zohar, then a spirit of goodness goes with him. However, when evil is done, "he draws upon himself another spirit which leads him astray to an evil side."[27] The body, teaches the Talmud, is the "scabbard of the soul."[28] Of man, said R. Meshullam, a medieval poet, "thou . . . didst breathe into him a pure soul from thy own heaven."[29]

יד

Man, said one sage, Bahya ibn Paquda, must approach existence "for the sake of heaven, for the sake of His great Name."[30] The heart, Dylan cries out in "FOREVER YOUNG," must be joyful, must discern the divine even where it is hidden from our sight. "Give me thy heart," God tells man (Proverbs 23:26). To illustrate such a thought, the Talmud teaches that, above David's bed, there hung a harp. With the arrival of midnight, a north wind would come ("North wind about to break," says Dylan in "NEVER SAY GOODBYE") and blow upon the harp, which would then play by itself for hours.[31] What melodies did such a stringed instrument play? Perhaps only the songs we have in our hearts, but which need planet waves to set the chords into motion. "And it came to pass, when the minstrel played, that the hand of the Lord came upon him." (Second Kings 3:15). Obtain the truth, teaches Scripture, but "sell it not" (Proverbs 23:23)—even where it is outlawed ("DIRGE").

Teaches Rabbi Heschel, of blessed memory: "A lie may be defined as an attempt to deceive without the other's consent. This definition assumes that there is a silent contract among men to speak the truth. Correct as this assumption is on one level, it is occasionally challenged on another. Publicly we all pay homage to honesty; privately, however, we rarely resent flattery. We are indignant when we are fooled by others but live comfortably with our unconscious desire for self-deceit, being effusive when we flatter our own selves, deriving pleasure from wishful

26. Philip Birnbaum, *Machzor Ha-Shalem*, "Evening Service for Yom Kippur," p. 528.

27. Zohar III, 86a.

28. (Babylonian Talmud), Sanhedrin 108a.

29. R. Meshullam, quoted, Philip Birnbaum, *Machzor Ha-Shalem*, "Additional Service for Yom Kippur," p. 812.

30. Bahya Ibn Paquda, *Hovot ha-Levavot*, ed. Haymson, part iv, p. 68.

31. (Babylonian Talmud), Berakot 3b.

thinking. *Mundus vult decipi*: the world wants to be deceived."[32]

יה

The poet, having smelled and tasted the asphyxiation of chaos, struggles with the limitations of language to tell us his heart's pathways in *Planet Waves*. Like Jeremiah (10:10), he has learned that God is a living God, that man must not "be dismayed at the signs of heaven" (10:2). We sense God's love, we strive to find His justice in a world gone mad. We stop and discover that, above all, God is truth. "It is the mystery of being," Rabbi Heschel has said. "Therefore, the way that always leads to God is truth. Yet truth is buried and remains hidden. In a world full of falsehood, Truth can survive only in concealment, for lies lie in wait everywhere. As soon as Truth is disclosed, it is surrounded by forces seeking to destroy it . . . *The test of Truth can take place only through the soul's confrontation with God,* in moments of disregard for self-regard, confronting one-self as one is confronted by God. The result is not an arbitrary private judgment. One is overcome by the certainty that to express God's existence is like affirming the existence of other human beings."[33]

Existence of other human beings—as it is for them, so it is for the poet: dualistic, walking the shadowy gray alleys between darkness and light. "You're the soul of many things," he calls out ("SOMETHING THERE IS ABOUT YOU"). He cries out against the lies one can tell another: "But to you that would be cruelty / And to me it surely would be death." The specter of death, the spiritual extinction of ideas and dreams, drums nervous fingers against the windows of the mind, which is often half-covered by the Venetian blinds erected between the mind and its own inner essence.

The Kotzker Rebbe (died 1859), that enigmatic Hasidic articulator of despair and release, once told a disciple: "I am not worried

32. A. J. Heschel, *A Passion For Truth*, p. 159.
33. *Ibid.*, pp. 164, 165.

With Phil Ochs at the benefit for Chile concert, May 1974.

CHUCK PULIN

VERNON SHIBLA

about hunger; what worries me is human cruelty."[34] In conforming to static structures of thought, we deform the soul. One day a Hasidic rabbi was told someone died of hunger. "No," said the rabbi, "he died of pride."[35] Hunger, pride, death: the world of illusions which flicker and dance before the soul in demonic frenzy, is both the adversary and the source of the poet's perceptions. "He's hungry, like a man in drag," Dylan once said ("TEMPORARILY LIKE ACHILLES"). Enveloping the soul with lies will precipitate destruction; but facing the truth can reintegrate one with one's being, can lead one from "deep in poverty" to giving of the soul ("WEDDING SONG"). Spiritual poverty surrounds the soul with a shell of indifference, but joy can break down the walls. "May your hands always be busy," teaches the poet ("FOREVER YOUNG"); may we taste "the labor of thy hands" (Psalm 128:2), the "fullness thereof" (Psalm 24:1). We mix medicine ("SUBTERRANEAN HOMESICK BLUES," "STUCK INSIDE OF MOBILE"), strangling our minds with neon, but "Healing comes from the Most High . . . The Lord has created medicines out of the earth . . ."[36]

Striving for completeness entails a reciprocal covenant between the poet and the divine, an avoidance of "suicide road" ("DIRGE") and desolation row. Yet we are not made of silver. "I have tried thee," it is written, "in the furnace of affliction" (Isaiah 48:10). "This teaches," says the Talmud, "that the Holy One, blessed be He, went through all the virtues in order to bestow them upon Israel and found none more becoming than poverty."[37] Why? Struggle for the poet means that the path to inner peace must be renewed with struggle. "And the land shall not be sold in perpetuity; for the land is Mine; for ye are strangers and settlers with Me" (Leviticus 25:23).

The subterfuges of despair extenuate the desire for peace; planet waves beat softly, then rage with typhoon intensity, *via solitaria*. A ladder is built ("A HARD RAIN'S A-GONNA FALL," "FOREVER YOUNG") to the soul's essence, and "all souls descend a ladder from Heaven to earth. Once they have arrived, the ladder is removed. But then the

souls are bidden to mount upward; they are called again and again. So they go about looking for the ladder . . . Some people give up, for how can one ascend to Heaven without a ladder?"[38] The ladder is *within* —and the *sefirot*, the emanations of God, are the rungs for ascension, for the parabolicism of Jewish consciousness. God is not only incomparable to anything man may erect as a stone shadow (see Isaiah 40:25), but He is also strength and song (note Exodus 15:2). He "will make darkness light" (Isaiah 42:16), the blind seeing (Isaiah 42:18). Thus, within *Planet Waves*, one encounters not *horror religiosus*; rather the poet shares the knowledge which comes from having been afflicted.

God *gives* faith to man. In darkened forests, cluttered with the junkyards of broken wings and walls of glass, our eyes search for Hebrew letters, for incantations with which to illumine our hidden paths, with which we can sing our songs ("FOREVER YOUNG"). Sing unto Him a new song," it is taught (Psalm 33:3), and on the appearance of the sun we call out: "declare Thy loving-kindness in the morning" (Psalm 92:2; compare to "NEW MORNING"). God and man now search for one another, opening doors and, in low whispers, the names of souls are carved in still air. We petition God, He calls out to us; but man, that child of elves and ships with wings, often refuses to hear the calling. We learn to love more than madness ("WEDDING SONG"), even when in an existence lamented by the Psalmist: "Mine adversaries taunt me; / While they say unto me all the day: 'Where is thy God?' " (Psalm 42:11). In the thunderous madness of "reality," the poet strives for rare moments of solitude, where the Doom Machine's *odium generis humani* is only a far-off echoing. He stands, with swift

---

34. quoted, *ibid.*, p. 167.

35. J. K. K. Rokotz, *Siach Sarfei Kodesh* (Lodz, 1929), quoted in the *The Hasidic Anthology: Tales and Teachings of the Hasidim*, trans. Louis I. Newman and Samuel Spitz (New York: Schocken Books, 1963), p. 351.

36. "The Wisdom of Sirach" quoted from *The Apocrypha*, trans. Edgar J. Goodspeed (New York: Vintage Books, 1959), p. 295.

37. (Babylonian Talmud), Hagigah 9b.

38. A. J. Heschel, *A Passion For Truth*, p. 186.

feet ("FOREVER YOUNG"), appearing before us with his dreams, then disappearing. And the divine demands that we stand upon our feet (Ezekiel 2:1–5), seeing His voice, hearing the letters of His words. We ask for God's graciousness, for His mercy, for "the multitude of Thy compassions" (Psalm 51:3). And with alertness for deception, our soul sings for an existence away "from the pit" (Psalm 103:4).

We discover creation and re-creation; and, as Rabbi Heschel, of blessed memory, has written, we sometimes sense a "mysterious waiting,"[39] as if our entire existence is in expectation. The pusillanimous edifices of

truth and illusion seem to merge in the echo chambers of the world after Auschwitz. We hear Moses' plea: "Show me, I pray Thee, Thy glory" (Exodus 33:18). We hear God's answer: "And I will take away My hand, and thou shalt see My back; but My face shall not be seen" (Exodus 23:23). We affirm the existence of the heavens—yet they remain beyond finitude's reaches. And Bob Dylan —as all Jewish psalmists before—turns to man's existence, this earth which God gave "to the children of men" (Psalm 115:16). The Psalmist chants: "Thou rulest the proud swelling of the sea; / When the waves thereof arise, Thou stillest them" (Psalm 89:10).

Will ye not tremble at My presence?

Who have placed the sand for the bound of the sea,
An everlasting ordinance, which it cannot pass;
And though the waves thereof toss themselves, yet can they not prevail;
Though they roar, yet can they not pass over it.
—Jeremiah 5:22.

Thus do we hear the chanting of the Jewish Bob Dylan: "I love you . . . More than the waves upon the sea" ("WEDDING SONG").

Disbelief, it might be said, is spiritually unnatural; believing is an "urge" which, even in the depths of despair, claws against the walls of our self-imposed blindness. We

At the benefit for Chile concert, May, 1974, with (left) Julian Beck of The Living Theater, and (right) Daniel Ellsberg, center.

stand, trembling, next to what the Ba'al Shem Tov called "the deep abyss of evil."[40] And the Kotzker Rebbe (much of his teaching bearing startling similarities to Bob Dylan's "CHIMES OF FREEDOM") was to say: "I stand with one foot in the highest Heaven and the other in hell."[41] We are persuaded to seek God "while He may be found, / Call ye upon Him while He is near" (Isaiah 55:6). And when he cannot be found, when He is not near, then do we compose lamentations,

39. *Ibid.*, p. 259.
40. quoted, *ibid.*, p. 276.
41. quoted, *ibid.*

then do we sense, with Bob Dylan, the specter of doom.

ז״

In "KNOCKIN' ON HEAVEN'S DOOR," Dylan paints a picture of spiritual darkness, where it is "too dark to see." In "FOREVER YOUNG," he hopes (pleads) that we might see that spiritual light enveloping us. He echoes the Psalmist:

> Even the darkness is not too dark
> for Thee,
> But the night shineth as the day;
> The darkness is even as the light.
> —Psalm 139:12.

Dylan speaks, in "DIRGE," of the "hollow place" within the soul, where chaos is given a voice of shrieking tongues. Who is the giver of the voice? "I am the Lord . . . I form the light, and create darkness" (Isaiah 45:7). We cry out, questioning, affirming His presence in our existence, yet know that God is beyond our understanding, that our thoughts are not His Thoughts (Isaiah 55:8). Our suffering, however, is not endless; in hearing and answering the call of God to man, a covenant is formulated. "In all their affliction He was afflicted, / And the angels of His presence saved them" (Isaiah 63:9). "Silence," said the Kotzker Rebbe, "is the greatest cry in the world . . . When a man has reason to scream, and cannot though he wants to—he has achieved the greatest scream."[42] And he was fond of quoting a parable (which is similar to Dylan's usage of "ladder to the star . . . climb on every rung," in "FOREVER YOUNG"): "Three ways are open to a man who is in sorrow. He who stands on a normal rung weeps, he who stands higher is silent, but he who stands on the topmost rung converts his sorrow into song."[43]

The spidery shadow of Auschwitz's smokestacks hovers over the words delivered to our souls by Dylan.

---

42. quoted, *ibid.*, p. 281.
43. quoted, *ibid.*, p. 283.

Dylan and Dave Van Ronk backstage at the benefit for Chile concert.

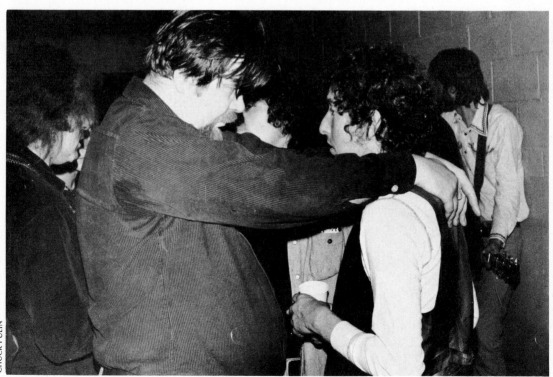

CHUCK PULIN

We are children of chaos; and the genitals of metallic precision ache and throb, yearning to have an orgasm with our fear. In the silence, we grope for words, formulations, incantations. "Thou didst turn for me my mourning into dancing," says the poet (Psalm 30:12). "Yes, to dance beneath the diamond sky," says yet another poet ("MR. TAMBOURINE MAN"), who has added: "May your heart always be joyful, / May your song always be sung" ("FOREVER YOUNG"). Another poet shouted his hopes: "Let them sing for joy upon their beds" (Psalm 149:5). "Wisdom," it is said, "is as unattainable to a fool as corals; / He openeth not his mouth in the gate" (Proverbs 24:7; compare "fool" to its usage in "STUCK INSIDE OF MOBILE"; and "gate" as the mystical symbol of "GATES OF EDEN"). "In faith," Rabbi Heschel, of blessed memory, tells us, "we can accept that there is *meaning beyond absurdity*, meaning which is *supra rationem*, above reason, not *contra rationem*, against reason . . . God is truth. We carry out His orders, pour water into leaking barrels, believing in the activity for its own sake. Is it conceivable that God Who is Truth would be deceiving us? Truth cannot lie—there can be no doubt about that. There *is* meaning, though it is concealed from us. Truth is buried, and so, too, is meaning."[44]

The poet blesses, before receiving; in need, we learn, first, to give to him.

יה

The poets, say the Jewish mystics, are recipients of gifts denied to angels. We learn to be strong "when the winds of changes shift" ("FOREVER YOUNG"), learn that angels are sometimes winds (Psalm 104:14). We seek, teaches the Zohar, to "penetrate right through to the soul, the root principle of all . . . the soul of the soul."[45]

Planet Waves is, indeed, "searching thru the ruins for a glimpse of Buddah (sic)," as Dylan writes in his liner notes. A glimpse of the divine within, a brief touch of the *Shekhinah*'s emanations, is a path all may take—but never alone, says the Talmud. Dylan has shared with us, in all of his released (and unre-

leased) poetry, perspectives of his spiritual path as a Jew, but he has not (as no poet can) given us "directions" for our own paths. Not only is Bob Dylan (the Jew, the father, the poet) a survivor of chaos' clasps—he is, also, the creator of his path. He once asked if we could crawl from our windows. So we must ask *within* ourselves . . . we must turn to the Talmud and its commentaries, to the Hasidim, to the kabbalah, to Jacob's ladder, to all of these—within our souls—as Bob Dylan has done. "May God bless and keep you always," he calls out to us.

> If I am I because I am I, and you are you because you are you, then I am I and you are you. However, if I am I because you are you, and you are you because I am I, then I am not I and you are not you.
> —the Kotzker Rebbe.[46]

All songs on *Planet Waves* published by and copyright © Ram's Horn Music, 1973 and 1974. A short version of this review appeared in *Fusion*, April-May 1974.

44. Ibid., pp. 288, 291.
45. Zohar III, 152a.
46. quoted, A. J. Heschel, *A Passion For Truth*, p. 144.

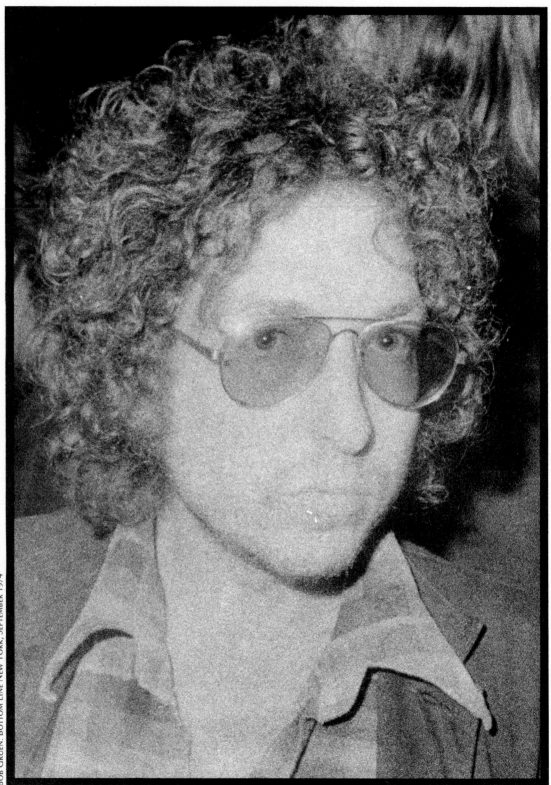

BOB GRUEN, BOTTOM LINE NEW YORK, SEPTEMBER 1974